101 Ways to Find A GHOST

101 Ways

to Find A

GHOST

Essential Tools, Tips, and Techniques
to **Uncover Paranormal Activity**

MELISSA MARTIN ELLIS

adamsmedia
AVON, MASSACHUSETTS

Published by
Adams Media, a division of F+W Media, Inc.
57 Littlefield Street, Avon, MA 02322. U.S.A.
www.adamsmedia.com

Contains material adapted and abridged from *The Everything® Ghost Hunting Book*
by Melissa Martin Ellis, copyright © 2009 by F+W Media, Inc.,
ISBN 10:1-59869-920-2, ISBN 13: 978-1-59869-920-3.

ISBN 10: 1-4405-1224-8
ISBN 13: 978-1-4405-1224-7
eISBN 10: 1-4405-1256-6
eISBN 13: 978-1-4405-1256-8

Printed in the United States of America.

10   9   8   7   6   5   4   3   2   1

Library of Congress Cataloging-in-Publication Data
is available from the publisher.

This publication is designed to provide accurate and authoritative information with regard to the subject matter covered. It is sold with the understanding that the publisher is not engaged in rendering legal, accounting, or other professional advice. If legal advice or other expert assistance is required, the services of a competent professional person should be sought.
—From a *Declaration of Principles* jointly adopted by a Committee of the American Bar Association and a Committee of Publishers and Associations

Many of the designations used by manufacturers and sellers to distinguish their product are claimed as trademarks. Where those designations appear in this book and Adams Media was aware of a trademark claim, the designations have been printed with initial capital letters.

Readers are urged to take all appropriate precautions before undertaking any how-to task. Always read and follow instructions and safety warnings for all tools and materials, and call in a professional if the task stretches your abilities too far. Although every effort has been made to provide the best possible information in this book, neither the publisher nor the author are responsible for accidents, injuries, or damage incurred as a result of tasks undertaken by readers. This book is not a substitute for professional services.

This book is available at quantity discounts for bulk purchases.
For information, please call 1-800-289-0963.

CONTENTS

Part 1. BE PREPARED: THINGS TO KEEP IN MIND   1

1. The Qualities Exemplified by a Ghost Hunter   1

2. Your Essential Equipment List   3

3. Keeping Accurate Records   6

4. Your Paranormal Self-Education   8

5. Building and Organizing a Team   11

6. Joining an Established Paranormal Research Group   13

7. Follow Strict Protocols to Protect Credibility   16

8. Following the Scientific Method   18

9. Instinct Versus Intellect   19

Part 2. GHOSTS, SPIRITS, AND ENTITIES: HAUNTS AND HOTSPOTS   23

10. Ghosts in Ancient Cultures   24

11. Who's Who?   26

12. What Are Ghosts Made Of? 30

13. Do My Eyes Deceive Me? 32

14. Where and What? 33

15. Residual Hauntings 35

16. Intelligent and Human Hauntings 38

Part 3. IN THE FIELD: PRACTICAL SKILLS AND WORK ON LOCATION 41

17. An Investigator's Common Sense Checklist 42

18. Doing a Walk-Through and Site Check with the Client 43

19. Equipment Check and Deployment 46

20. Recording Data and Observations Manually 47

21. Client Interviews and Collecting Eyewitness Accounts 48

22. Confidentiality and Protecting the Client's Privacy 51

23. Educating and Comforting Clients 54

24. Making an Honest Assessment: Is It Worth Investigating? 56

25. Integrity and Accountability to Clients 57

26. Showing the Data to the Client 59

27. Following Up   61

28. Extended Investigations and Repeat Offenders   62

29. The Client's Responsibility   63

30. Remaining Objective and Professional   64

Part 4. ANALYSIS AND REVIEW OF EVIDENCE   67

31. Evaluating the Evidence   68

32. Hard Evidence Versus Personal Experiences   69

33. Analyzing the Evidence   70

34. What to Look For   71

35. Being Aware of Matrixing Anomalies   72

36. Reviewing Photos and Video   74

37. Evidence Preservation and Preparation   76

38. CD or DVD Digital Storage   77

Part 5. PSYCHIC SKILLS: SENSITIVE TO THE SUPERNATURAL   81

39. Intuition or Coincidence?   82

40. Tapping the Source   83

41. Types of Psychic Abilities   84

42. Psychics and Seers   85

43. Necromancy: Talking with the Dead   87

44. Map Dowsing   89

45. Scrying   92

Part 6. SELF-DEFENSE AND PROTECTION   95

46. Basic Protection   96

47. Invoking St. Michael   97

48. When the Hunter Becomes the Hunted   98

49. Psychic Attack   99

50. Dealing with Psychic Oppression   102

51. Potential Damage from Malevolent Entities   103

52. Physical Attack   104

53. Client or Problematic People Issues   107

54. Guarding Against Equipment Failure   108

55. Jinxes and Hexes   109

56. Possession   111

57. Calling in Priests and Clergy   112

58. Wards, Shields, and Visualization   114

59. Using Sigils and Charms   116

60. Cleansing Techniques and Rituals   117

Part 7. INVESTIGATIVE WORK: RESEARCH AND LEGALITIES   123

61. Handling a Request to Investigate   124

62. Assessing the Threat Level   125

63. The On-Site Interview   126

64. Understanding the Site Layout and Location 129

65. Inform Yourself about the Site Beforehand   131

66. Resources for Background Searches   133

67. Other Sources of Site Information and History   135

68. Basic Forms for Investigations   137

69. Permission and Release Forms   139

70. Securing Permission to Access a Site   141

71. Permission-Free Sites   146

72. Medical Information and Preparedness   146

73. Getting Insurance and Covering Your Assets   150

Part 8. GEAR AND TECHNOLOGY   153

74. Ghost Hunting in the Digital Age   154

75. Paranormal Investigation Gear   154

76. Video and Still Photography   156

77. Audio Voice Recorders and Electronic Voice Phenomena   157

78. Thermometers and Chilly Spirits   160

79. Infrared and Thermal Imaging Cameras   161

80. EMF and ELF Meters   162

81. Low-Tech Tools: Flashlights, Lanterns, Compasses, and Watches   166

82. Miscellaneous Other Equipment   167

83. Practical Clothing   170

84. Capturing Electronic Voice Phenomena   171

85. White Noise and the Ghost Box   174

86. Capturing Elusive Images   176

Part 9. TEAMWORK   179

87. A Team Leader's Accountability to Team Members   180

88. Two Key Team Positions: Case Manager and Equipment Manager   182

89. Reports: Logging a Case from Start to Finish   184

90. Awareness, Responsibility, and Safety   186

91. Working with Sensitives on the Team   188

92. Photographers and Videographers   191

93. Parapsychologists and Demonologists   192

Part 10. GHOST HUNTING AS A HOBBY OR PROFESSION   195

94. Hobbyist or Professional?   196

95. Tips on Maintaining a Professional Reputation   199

96. Using Rigorous Methodology   200

97. Evidence Standards: Applying Scientific Methodology   201

98. Using the Internet for Research and Promotion   203

99. The Importance of Networking   205

100. Sharing and Expanding Your Knowledge   206

101. Beyond Seeking Evidence of the Supernatural   209

Appendix A: Most Haunted Sites in America   213

Appendix B: Famous Ghosts 217

Appendix C: Glossary 221

Appendix D: Bibliography 231

Index 235

Part 1

BE PREPARED: THINGS TO KEEP IN MIND

Whether you are a believer or a skeptic, ghost hunting can be a totally fascinating experience that blends aspects of spiritualism, adventure, and science. If you are interested in the world of spirits and have asked the age-old question, "Does the soul continue after death?" you may have what it takes to be a ghost hunter . . . and you are in good company.

A ghost hunter, also known as a paranormal investigator, seeks to collect data concerning paranormal activity in places reported to be haunted. The general goal is to investigate, research, and document evidence of paranormal activity.

If being a ghost hunter interests you (either professionally or as a hobby), you've come to the right place! This book will help you get started.

1. The Qualities Exemplified by a Ghost Hunter

To become a paranormal investigator or ghost hunter, you must have some great qualities: objectivity, patience, courage, strength of character, and total honesty. However, both believers and nonbelievers must also have the ability to suspend their judgment long enough to gauge all of the facts objectively. Be sure you're emotionally ready to obtain tangible knowledge about the other side should you find evidence to support it. The reverse is also true. Today's ghost hunters know that investigation of paranormal phenomena should be approached seriously, with respect and caution. This is not a parlor game or fun party activity.

The best investigators in the psychic world are those who have actively cultivated patience and reliability. The individual who is calm, mature, and patient brings stability and credibility to the investigation. These qualities are vital when dealing with a panicky client in a state of high anxiety. You should cultivate patience and reliability not only for your own good, but also for the sake of your colleagues and clients. By its very nature, the paranormal field is full of chaotic activity and confusion. You, as the person brought into the situation to resolve the scary issues and answer the difficult questions, must be an absolute rock of stability and confidence. Remember that people who come to you for help may be scared or angry, and they may unconsciously direct their emotions at you; don't take their aggression personally. You might also want to look into methods of physical and mental relaxation and focus, such as yoga or meditative techniques such as concentrative meditation, mindfulness meditation, or breathing meditation. All these can help you learn to manage your emotional state, which can help you in dealing with clients as well as working in stressful situations on-site while investigating.

Keep a skeptical but open mind as you explore th natural realm. As scientist Rupert Sheldrake says, "Healthy skepticism plays an important part in science, and stimulates research and critical thinking. Healthy skeptics are open-minded and interested in evidence. By contrast, dogmatic skeptics are committed to the belief that 'paranormal' phenomena are impossible, or at least so improbable as to merit no serious attention. Hence any evidence for such phenomena must be illusory."

Your credibility as a paranormal investigator relies on maintaining your objectivity. Critics and skeptics believe that most ghost hunters are unreliable. Ghost hunters are often labeled fantasy-prone personalities—people who like to make things up.

Although the skeptic's analysis of the facts about ghost hunters may seem a bit skewed, it does underscore the importance of paranormal investigators being totally professional and reliable in the course of their work.

Your standard operating procedure should include keeping scrupulous records and honoring client commitments and confidentiality while looking for normal everyday explanations of phenomena.

2. Your Essential Equipment List

What are the must-have pieces of equipment for ghost hunting?

+ *A flashlight and extra batteries.* It is not unusual for a flashlight to go out during an investigation. Some believe paranormal entities cause such devices to stop working. The theory posits that entities try to manifest by drawing energy from their immediate environment and will often drain even brand-new batteries within minutes.

+ *A first-aid kit.* As you're walking around in old buildings in pitch darkness, be prepared to deal with a few scratches, bumps, and scrapes.

+ *A notebook and pencil or pen.* Old-fashioned writing devices are vital for keeping track of observations and sequences of events.

+ *A watch.* Invest in an old-fashioned wind-up watch that doesn't run on batteries. If possible, get one with a second hand.

+ *A tape recorder.* It can be either analog or digital, but it must have an external microphone that can be placed away from the recorder to minimize static and noise.

+ *A camera.* It can be a digital or film camera, but it should have a flash so that you have the option to use it or not. Bring extra camera batteries. (For detailed information on photographic equipment, accessories, and uses, see Chapter 76.)

+ *An electromagnetic frequency (EMF) meter.* This new ghost-hunting tool measures the electromagnetic field in the area. (For detailed information on EMF meters, their use, and where to obtain one, see Chapter 80.)

+ *A cell phone.* They often don't function well in paranormal hot spots, but bring one anyway, just in case you need to make contact with other team members or to call for help. Never go into the field alone or without telling someone else where your team will be and when you plan to be back.

Other less essential, inexpensive, low-tech items you might put in your ghost-hunting kit include the following:

- *Candles and matches or a kerosene lantern.* These are a good backup in case the flashlight goes dead.
- *A pendulum.* This is an ancient way of communicating with spirits.
- *Dowsing rods.* These are used by some in the same way as an EMF meter.
- *Rubber cement and black string.* These can be tacked across access points to detect whether someone is entering or leaving the site without your knowledge.
- *A magnetic anomaly detector* to gauge the presence of magnetic field anomalies, which can sometimes indicate the presence of unusual paranormal activity.
- *A tape measure or yardstick* to measure any object that may appear to have moved from its former position.
- *A map of the area* to acquaint yourself and your team with the site's layout.

The most important things to bring to an investigation are your common sense, your sensitivity and investigative skills, and a buddy. Never go into the field alone; you could end up hurt or trapped somewhere.

3. Keeping Accurate Records

You must take good notes to keep track of unusual phenomena, even if someone is simultaneously videotaping the investigation. Notes can be a valuable way of recording important data; the camera can't catch every angle at once, nor can it know what you have just experienced on a personal level—an impression, a cold spot, or a ghostly touch. Keeping a written record of your reactions to things that happen can help you reconstruct the investigation later.

Here are some things to keep in mind when you take notes and document your research:

* Make a note of anything you think is significant. Record any possible ordinary explanations. For example, if you detect a drop in temperature, a potential non-supernatural explanation is a poorly insulated room or an approaching change in weather.
* Later, eliminate all events or discrepancies that seem to be suspect and that may have ordinary explanations.
* List the remaining items separately, in order of significance, to ensure clarity of thought and to help you arrange your list logically.
* Don't discard less significant facts. Instead, move them to the bottom and be aware that their status can change as the investigation proceeds.
* Never ignore the influence of random coincidence. Most investigations involve some elements of coincidence or randomness.

When you analyze your data, seek meaning abilities and correlations from the facts in orde. ... ... the amount of guesswork in your analyses and conclusions. Dispassionately reviewing the evidence, both from your own personal experiences and from the electronic voice phenomena recordings, digital video recordings (DVRs), and even digital thermometer readings, will help you make a balanced assessment that can withstand the scrutiny of critics and debunkers.

Keep a log during the investigation. These go by different names, such as paranormal investigation log, paranormal investigator's logbook, and paranormal vigil log. Whatever they are called, these notebooks help keep track of important investigation data and serve as reference points if anything anomalous happens. They also contain the investigator's record of the equipment used and readings from that equipment.

A good logbook should have space to record:

- Weather conditions, temperature, barometric pressure
- EMF field activity
- The moon phase
- Sunspot activity
- Equipment checklist
- Equipment used on specific investigations, plus baseline readings
- Remarkable investigative events
- Anomalous personal experiences
- Personal contact information, including emergency contact information, medications, and medical information

Even the simplest logs should contain a column where the investigator's own impressions, perceptions, and any potential paranormal incidents are noted. If an investigator's hair is pulled, if she smells roses, if she receives the impression of a voice, or if she sees an apparition, it must be noted on this paper so it can be used to correlate data between investigators and locations.

4. Your Paranormal Self-Education

If you decide you want to pursue a career as a paranormal investigator, either as a hobby or as a profession, you need to gather a library of reference materials and educate yourself about the many sorts of unexplained phenomena and hauntings. Bookstores and online sources such as Amazon.com make these reference materials, magazines, books, and websites available to everyone.

If you have an inquiring and open mind, you have a very fascinating experience ahead of you. There is much to learn and much to explore. In addition, what you learn will change how you view the world, yourself, and the people around you.

So where should you begin? Picking up a book is a good, basic way to start.

+ The occult books by British author Colin Wilson are very thorough and insightful. *Mysteries*, *The Occult*, and *Poltergeist* are particularly recommended.

+ D. Scott Rogo's *The Welcoming Silence: A Study of Psychical Phenomena and Survival of Death* and *Haunted House Handbook* offer good overviews of the subject.
+ Loyd Auerbach's *ESP, Hauntings and Poltergeists* is another excellent work for people seeking an overview.

As you read books on the paranormal, keep paper and pen handy to take notes on ideas and concepts that you find of particular interest or would like to follow up on.

Although you can perform research on the Internet, make sure the sites you look at have some sort of credibility and the people involved are individuals with a background in, respect for, and history within the paranormal community. Try to learn which websites have long histories of credibility and which organizations have been around for many years and have proven themselves. The Atlantic Paranormal Society (TAPS) website (*www.the-atlantic-paranormal-society.com*) has a great deal of information, as does Troy Taylor's (*www.prairieghosts.com/abtauthor.html*) and The Rhode Island Paranormal Research Group's (T.R.I.P.R.G.; *www.triprg.com/index1.htm*).

Although reading and research can prepare paranormal investigators for the possibilities of ghost hunting, taking actual classes can better help you grasp subtleties and procedures. They are also useful for learning the technical aspects of the business, such as how to properly operate an EMF meter and how to handle an EVP (electronic voice phenomena, recorded noises that resemble speech but aren't intentionally recorded voices) investigation.

Any class you take should cover the following information:

+ How to locate haunted sites
+ How to research the site's history
+ How to interview eyewitness
+ How to build a ghost-hunting kit
+ How to record EVPs
+ How to use EMF meters and digital thermometers
+ How to use a digital camera in the investigation
+ How to form a team or paranormal group

This information should be covered whether you take an online class, home-study class, or a class at a continuing education institution. Sign up for classes only after you have checked out the credentials of the instructors and institutions.

You should double check all classes, particularly Internet classes. If the quality of the classes or the institution is subpar, you can easily get feedback from other students.

If you live in Connecticut, Rhode Island, or Massachusetts, you may be within easy driving distance of The Atlantic Paranormal Society (TAPS)'s one-day seminars and lectures. TAPS is the organization featured on the Syfy Channel's *Ghost Hunters* TV show. Although the cost of their workshops is generally very reasonable ($40 for a one-day seminar), they sell out very quickly.

Online classes vary widely in cost. Classes priced at $100 are at the high end of the scale. Flamel College (*www .flamelcollege.org*) offers a paranormal investigator certification for $99. This fee includes an EMF meter. Universal

Class (*www.universalclass.com*) has a very reasonably priced ($20) online class for beginning investigators. With certification, it is $45.

Fiona Broome, the founder of Hollow Hill (*www.hollowhill.com*), a ghost hunters' website, offers classes in different levels so students can take classes appropriate to their situation. Her courses are offered on CDs.

Maybe a conference is more along the lines of what you're looking for. Some ghost-hunting groups organize annual getaways held over two or more days with workshops, ghost tours, paranormal investigations, and media presentations. Type "ghost hunter conference" into an Internet search engine and see what comes up.

5. Building and Organizing a Team

The start-up investigator may decide to ask a few like-minded friends to form a paranormal group. Set a few rules and create a system for doing investigations early on. Things run more smoothly if everyone in the group understands the basic theories behind paranormal anomalies and has done some of the recommended readings.

Usually, the group breaks down into teams of two and they disperse to various areas that need to be investigated. Pair people whose investigative styles are similar and whose skills complement one another. This sort of partnership is optimal, and a great deal more can be accomplished if the investigators' personalities mesh well. Nothing is worse than pairing people who get on each other's nerves or bicker about procedures. Team leaders who have to deal with this sort of thing grow very frustrated in dealing with human issues rather than paranormal ones. The energy the investigators bring to a case can affect the outcome and radically change the course of the case, so take care to choose members who are mature enough to put ego aside and work well with others.

As the popularity of investigating the paranormal grows, most groups are inundated with new member requests. At first, this may seem like a good thing, but you must screen and assess new members before you invite them to be a part of your team. Being a paranormal investigator is not for everyone. It requires a rare combination of traits (objectivity, patience, and courage, to name just a few), the drive to explore the unknown, an unquenchable curiosity, and a mature and responsible approach to the field. Choosing members wisely is as important as training them well, so design a form to screen out thrill seekers and the unstable or irresponsible. Which questions will help you achieve those ends is up to each individual group, but each application should include questions about the prospective member's education and employment history and hypothetical situations that test the applicant's common sense.

Make sure the people that you bring together communicate clearly and volunteer information. If you have to drag it out of them or constantly ask for clarification, chances are good they'll withhold critical information while on assignment or during evidence review, as well. Those attracted to the paranormal definitely march to a different drummer, so is it any wonder they shy away from talking about all the mundane day-to-day business that may be involved in their otherwise exciting endeavors? However, if investigators are not able to clearly communicate, they won't get very far or enjoy the investigations as much as they might have otherwise, and may in fact hold the investigation back.

6. Joining an Established Paranormal Research Group

Sometimes the hardest part of the hunt is finding people with whom to work or train.

Joining an established group is really the best way to get the proper training and learn the many skills you will need as a paranormal investigator. Ask about paranormal groups that meet regularly in your community. Try to find individuals who have developed a reputation as psychic or paranormal investigators. You can also use the Internet. Do a search using the name of your town or area and the words "ghost hunters." You may find there is an established group nearby.

When you locate a team you're interested in joining, call or write and introduce yourself. Set up an appointment to meet them and see if you can arrange to go on a ghost hunt. Most people in the paranormal field are very friendly souls. They are in the business of helping other people in trouble, usually at their own expense, so they are likely to be receptive to sincere overtures.

Most groups that perform paranormal investigations have a form they ask new members to fill out. They do this to be sure you understand the responsibilities, possible danger, and/or legal issues involved in paranormal investigation. This form frees them from legal liability should anything happen to you in the course of the investigation. You will also be briefed on the group's procedures and investigative techniques. It is likely you will be put on probation until the training is completed. This is to ensure that you understand all the possible ramifications of your actions should something unexpected occur.

These groups do actively screen out people with mental problems and those who abuse drugs and alcohol. Smoking is not allowed during investigations for several reasons: It can be a fire hazard in old structures, and smoke can be mistaken for paranormal mists or fog.

People are also trained to keep their religious opinions to themselves. It is inevitable that people on an investigation may begin to discuss the afterlife and the question of life after death. This sort of discussion is acceptable, but when it crosses the line into a discussion of an individual's religious beliefs it can lead to discord and dissension in the group.

A good organization should expose you to and train you in the tools of the trade as they are defined today. You may have an affinity for one particular tool, say a dowsing rod or digital camera. If you find that you're particularly adept at something, try to develop your expertise in it; the group will appreciate having someone who is highly skilled and motivated. No two researchers are the same, and everyone's skill levels will vary.

A calm demeanor and good observational skills are essential to any paranormal researcher. If you can remain objective and are keenly aware of your surroundings, you will be an invaluable asset to any group you join. If you have any natural psychic ability, you can work on developing your sensitivity and skills in that area. A sort of natural on-the-job training in this area occurs as a result of the feedback you receive on an investigation.

Initially, you will probably work with an experienced investigator to gather eyewitness accounts. Carefully observe the sorts of questions that are asked. Just as important, note the way they are asked. Some organizations will do a preliminary interview with a potential client to see if a full-scale investigation is warranted. An experienced team member usually evaluates the information supplied. A walk-through of the property may be done at this time as well. Some groups bring a psychic along to the preliminary interviews to see if any paranormal activity can be detected, particularly if the person who contacted the group mentions that there may be a poltergeist or harmful activity that may threaten the safety or well-being of those who occupy or work at the site. This holds especially true if there are children on the premises. Every effort must be made to speed the investigation along if the well-being of children is at stake.

A WORD OF CAUTION

Some so-called paranormal investigation groups are actually scammers. Their primary goal is to frighten the client into believing that certain items in their home are haunted or possessed and must be removed immediately. These items are usually antiques or other valuables that are then sold or pawned.

7. Follow Strict Protocols to Protect Credibility

More and more groups are adopting strict protocols for ghost hunting. It is rare to find a group today that completely ignores the scientific approach in favor of the barging-around-an-old-house approach of yesteryear. Groups who do so quickly find themselves without clients and faced with genuine credibility issues.

With the scientific approach, the investigators seek to gather and follow the evidence, only declaring the incident paranormal when all the natural explanations have been discarded. Sometimes this is at odds with investigations that seek neither to foster nor debunk mysteries but only to solve them. The methods may vary slightly from group to group, but those seeking hard evidence of a haunting must necessarily follow similar rules to achieve their ends. For example:

+ They obtain permission to visit the site, clearing it with whatever agency or person controls access.
+ They investigate in teams. Investigators buddy up so no one is alone.
+ Strict records are kept of the equipment in use and electronic equipment is checked over before being used in the field to ensure its reliability.
+ The phenomenon that has been reported is analyzed for reproducibility by natural means.
+ Evidence is carefully screened and reviewed with the aim of debunking it.

♦ Evidence that cannot be debunked is properly archived and preserved.

The goal is to gather credible, reproducible evidence of life after death, communications from those who have passed on, poltergeist phenomena, or even malevolent hauntings. If any evidence is in doubt, it is discarded. This practice sometimes causes discord in a group. Some members may argue that the evidence is credible when others believe it is not. Groups will often set up evidence meetings where all members can examine evidence and vote on whether or not to keep it.

The scientific approach is a hard discipline to learn. Not all investigators see it as a good thing, especially when it emphasizes gathering evidence over helping the people who are being disturbed.

The best ghost hunters are the people who do not lose sight of why they got into the field in the first place—simply to help people. If tons of evidence is gathered on a case but the family has been driven out of their home, the case does not have a happy resolution.

Some of the most compelling events occur when an investigator has a personal encounter with a paranormal event. Unfortunately, if these personal experiences are not backed up by physical evidence in the form of a photo or recording, they are not considered hard evidence, even if another person was there to witness it. Information should be gathered using the scientific method:

1. Define the question. In a paranormal investigation this might be something like, "What is causing the unusual events as detailed by this client?"

2. Gather information and resources.
3. Form a hypothesis.
4. Perform experiments and collect data. At minimum, you'll need a camera, an audio recorder, a watch, and a notepad to do this.
5. Analyze data.
6. Interpret data and draw conclusions that serve as a starting point for a new hypothesis.
7. Publish results.
8. Always retest.

8. Following the Scientific Method

Perhaps the science of paranormal investigation can put an end to the misguided stereotypes of investigators as gullible and antiscientific. At last, ghost hunters are gaining credibility and being taken a bit more seriously. Yes, there are still many skeptics who claim what they do is pseudoscience, but as the evidence grows, people's minds will open.

For the field to gain credibility and respectability, investigators know they must do two things. First, they must discard evidence that could have a normal explanation. Second, they must follow the scientific method during investigations.

An investigator employing the scientific method must remain both open-minded and skeptical. Phenomena must be questioned. To get to the root cause, the scientific investigator must ask questions based on the scientific method:

+ Why is the event happening?
+ Is there a natural, root cause?
+ Is this incident connected to any other causative events?
+ Has other research or literature found connections between events you have observed?
+ Have other researchers drawn the same conclusions?
+ What is your hypothesis? Does it agree with your colleagues' hypotheses or is it new?
+ How will you test your hypothesis?
+ Can the hypothesis be tested under controlled conditions?
+ What predictions can be made based on the hypothesis?
+ Are tests based on the hypothesis statistically significant?

After all these steps, if the hypothesis is proven, you should publish your results in a reputable scientific journal. Other investigators will note the experimental protocols you used and they will try to reproduce your results. If your peers can repeat your experiments successfully, you may have come up with a new theory to explain the unexplained.

9. Instinct Versus Intellect

Many skeptics dismiss the whole topic of investigating the paranormal as a black-and-white issue of intellect versus instinct. However, you should never view intellect and instinct as conflicting with each other. As you pursue your paranormal studies and investigations, you will rely heavily on both qualities.

Your intellect and observational skills play a key role in your investigations. You should always look for a natural explanation for any observed or reported phenomenon before concluding that an event is paranormal in origin. Frankly, in most cases you will be able to find a mundane explanation when you examine the evidence thoroughly. As long ago as the nineteenth century, the Society for Psychical Research (SPR) began trying to debunk activity or explain it by natural means. Today's investigators have developed this approach toward the paranormal even further. It is a good one to follow.

But listening to your instinct is important, too. Instinct can tell you when a situation is potentially dangerous or lead you to a certain room or area where your investigation will bear fruit. The important thing is to keep a good balance between intellect and intuition.

As a paranormal investigator, you must learn to hone your observational skills to almost superhuman levels. When you have learned to use the equipment and mastered all the many dos and don'ts for effective field work, you still have to develop the skills you need to observe your surroundings with a truly critical eye. To do this, you must assess and observe the location objectively. Learn to release your emotions and let go of the preconceived ideas you have about a site or situation. First, consider the facts. Take a statement of unusual events from the client, then make your own observations and judgments of those events.

If you investigate long enough, you will inevitably encounter a circumstance that cannot be explained by any natural law or debunked by an everyday explanation. When this happens, it is important to maintain an open and alert state of mind. This is easily said, but hard to do. When the human mind is confronted by phenomena it cannot quickly categorize or readily understand, it tends to either freeze or race out of control. Your heart may pound and your thoughts may grow chaotic or confused.

So how do you cope with these reactions? The answer isn't a simple one; each individual has a different threshold for dealing with anxiety and fear. If you are a total skeptic, you may find that you completely shut down and simply refuse to process or believe what you are seeing. On the other hand, if you have a tendency to be open-minded, you may be better prepared to handle the situation. In either case, you should work with a partner and use technology to help you keep an objective record of the event. Try to maintain as professional a demeanor as you can, given the circumstances. In reality, ghost hunting is a subject open to enough ridicule and criticism already, so scrupulous investigation is required. That attitude builds not only the team's credibility, but it also brings higher standards to a field that really needs them.

Part 2

GHOSTS, SPIRITS, AND ENTITIES: HAUNTS AND HOTSPOTS

Perhaps the question is not *whether* something is out there but *what* is out there.

When people see ghosts, are they actually experiencing a form of mental telepathy? Are they seeing remnants of an event from the past that has been imprinted somehow on the surroundings? Or are they seeing the projection of a person who has died?

In most ancient cultures, ghosts were believed to be the restless spirits of the dead, seeking vengeance or attempting to complete unfinished business. Although they no longer had physical bodies, they could still manifest themselves, not only visually, but also through other sensory phenomena. They were able to move furniture, throw projectiles through walls, and create loud noises and other disruptions.

Credible witnesses over decades, even centuries, have reported seeing things that have no rational explanation according to the laws that govern the natural world. About 33 percent of Americans believe in ghosts and UFOs, and almost half—48 percent—believe in extrasensory perception, or ESP.

Most people who are interested in the paranormal are just average folks who have had an experience they cannot explain. An inexplicable experience changes a person's perception of the world; it leads them to search for answers. In essence, they become ghost hunters.

10. Ghosts in Ancient Cultures

Ghost stories are found in all cultures and all times, and the accounts of how ghosts look and behave is remarkably consistent. In the ancient world, ghosts were often seen as fog-like figures, made of subtle material, like the white mist exhaled in cold climates. Perhaps this is why the Latin word for "breath" is *spiritus*.

In the traditions of India, where belief in reincarnation is widespread, bereaved relatives sometimes followed an ancient ritual. At night, in a corner of the room where the deceased had slept, a saucer of water, rice, and ashes were placed on a sheet of white paper on the floor. No one was allowed to sleep in the room, and any kind of noise was forbidden.

It was believed that an imprint would appear in the ashes to foretell what would become of the deceased. If the imprint was a human baby's foot, the person would be reborn as a human. An Om imprint meant the person had gone to heaven and would not be reborn. An animal imprint meant the person would be reborn as an animal. If there was no imprint, it meant the person's spirit had not moved on. As the Garuda Purana, an ancient Hindu scripture, states, "All these are sure to be born as ghosts—a man misappropriating a trust property, a man treacherous to his friend, a man fond of another man's wife, a faithless man and a deceptive wretch."

The ancient Egyptian belief in the afterlife is described in *The Book of Going Forth by Day*, which is more commonly known as *The Book of the Dead*. It contains all the instructions that Egyptian royalty would need to make a comfortable transition to the afterlife. Those Egyptians who could afford the rites of beatification were assured an extenuation of their normal life on earth, full of banqueting and socializing. The dead could receive letters from the living and could visit them in dreams or visions to impart their wisdom.

Ghosts appear in many stories that have come down to us from ancient Greece, through such renowned storytellers as Pliny, Homer, and Virgil. Interwoven with tales of mythical gods and heroes, the ghosts of ancient Greece were very much a part of its culture. *The Odyssey* contains a long passage that describes the hero, Odysseus, going to the Underworld to talk to the shades of the dead, to find out what he should do next to return home. Circe tells him that he should travel past the groves of Persephone, where he will find the house of Hades, which is described as a place where the light of Helios (the sun) never shone. Circe instructs him in the rituals he must perform to fend off the shades of the dead until he is able to get the answers he seeks.

The ancient Romans celebrated Lemuria, a nine-day festival in May designed to soothe the harmful spirits, or *lemures*.

According to a passage in Ovid's poem *Fasti*, the festival was instituted to appease Remus, whose spirit haunted early Rome. The Romans apparently had three classifications for spirits. They were called *lares* if they were good, *lemures* if they were evil, and *manes* if their disposition was yet to be determined.

Often referred to as "the night-wandering shades of the prematurely dead," the lemures may have been souls who could find no peace, either because they had met with a violent death or had unfinished business. They wandered among the living, tormenting people and sometimes driving them to early deaths or madness. That rather sounds like the entities we call poltergeists.

During the ancient Roman festival of Parentalia and the feast of Feralia, held in February, the living descendants of benevolent and beloved spirits shared a meal with their honored ancestors. It was believed they watched over the welfare of the family along with the other household deities.

11. Who's Who?

Though the terms *ghost* and *apparition* are often used interchangeably, they are actually not the same type of entity at all. For example, *shadow people*, also called *shadow men* or *shadow beings*, are a type of apparition. They are often described as black humanoid silhouettes, usually without any details, although they are sometimes reported to have red or yellow eyes. Their movements are often said to be very jiggly and abnormal or extremely slow and slippery, like a liquid shadow.

Ghosts are more human in appearance, if they have a visual component. If you are visiting a historic site and glimpse someone in period garb, you would naturally assume you've seen a tour guide or that there is some other plausible explanation for the person's odd clothes. But if you saw that same person walk through a solid wall, or if no one else noticed him, you might begin to suspect that you had just seen a ghost.

A figure that is misty or partially transparent may be either a ghost or an apparition. But what if you see something so dark it looks as if it is made of shadows? Perhaps it is a demon.

A *demon* is a category of entity quite distinct from either a ghost or an apparition. There is also the added component of evil—a being that takes delight in tormenting the living. It implies a malicious and active type of haunting, which is quite different from a residual haunting—something like a taped version of an event that plays and replays over decades or even centuries. The entities in a haunting of this type do not seem to be aware of onlookers and don't interact with them in any way.

Demons, on the other hand, seem to want to interact; indeed, they seem to derive a lot of pleasure from doing so. Reports of these creatures predate the Bible, and accounts of them have existed in one form or another in every civilization of which we have a record. They were often simply called evil spirits. The word "demon" is derived from the Greek *daimon*, and in ancient Iran and India they were called *daewon*. These malevolent spirits were perceived as fallen angels in the Christian tradition. Whatever you call them, they are bad news. Dealing with these spirits requires preparation, an abundance of caution, and most definitely some outside help.

A *poltergeist* is a noisy spirit that makes its presence known primarily by way of sound. Physical manifestations follow, beginning as scratching noises from within the walls and escalating to more frequent banging or thumping sounds. Objects begin to sail through the air, usually narrowly missing the unfortunate inhabitants. Often, an adolescent or teenager lives in the house where the manifestations occur.

Adults can trigger the manifestations, too. All that is truly necessary is that the person be troubled emotionally. One theory is that this person may be unconsciously manipulating the items in the house by means of psychokinesis, the power to move things with an energy generated by the brain. Although largely unexplained, psychokinetic energy has been demonstrated to exist. Usually, people have no idea they are causing the poltergeist activity, which is happening all around them, and they are surprised to learn they themselves could be making the chaotic events happen.

Are ghosts and poltergeists the same thing? Actually, there is a bit of disagreement about this. Some investigators say they are different. Poltergeists are classified as nonhuman entities that produce destructive phenomena. They are capable of starting fires, rearranging furniture, throwing objects, and producing human-sounding voices and footsteps. Poltergeists are usually heard but not seen.

To be fair, not all cases of poltergeist activity involve troubled individuals; these hauntings aren't always so easily categorized. It is vital that the paranormal investigators involved be observant and not jump to conclusions too quickly. The typical poltergeist disturbance does not usually last long.

A POLTERGEIST CASE

Poltergeist disturbances usually subside after just a few weeks, although the malicious entity that tormented the Bell family between 1817 and 1821 was certainly a notable exception. The problems started for the Bells when they began hearing noises that sounded as if someone were pounding on the walls. Soon the Bells began to hear other sounds, such as scratching and knocking. This is a classic example of poltergeist phenomena. But instead of building to a crescendo and then diminishing, the phenomena increased. Soon physical attacks began; people were scratched, slapped, had their bedcovers ripped off, and were thrown out of bed. Although almost everyone in the household suffered similar treatment, the focus seemed to be on the Bells's daughter, Betsy. The terrifying activity in the Bell household went on for a long time and is very well documented; local legend has it that even General Andrew Jackson had an encounter.

Elementals are often described as primitive and malevolent beings or forces that attach themselves to a particular location. Elemental spirits are believed to be comprised of what the ancients perceived as the building blocks of the world—earth, air, fire, and water. Magicians and sorcerers believed they could use these spirits to do their bidding through a process called *binding*, which protected the person doing the spell from harm and allowed her to control the spirit as it did whatever task she assigned it. Today's dabblers in the occult occasionally try to control elementals, and can attest to the fact that the process of binding can backfire.

The entities in inhuman hauntings, such as demons or elementals, are powerful forces of unknown origin. One thing we do know is that these entities may try to harm or possess humans. They can be a serious threat, and have caused harm and even death. They are not in the same class as the entities of intelligent human hauntings, commonly called ghosts, or the memory remnants of the residual haunting. They are far more powerful and dangerous. You should steer clear of demons, intelligent hauntings with a score to settle, and sometimes even elementals. It is widely believed that ghosts can't harm you, but it is possible to sustain physical, mental, or emotional harm in the course of an investigation. Even paranormal investigators who have taken every safety precaution and forearmed themselves in every way should be prepared to meet an entity that will cause them to retreat. Be cautious, careful, and respectful. Be aware that on rare occasions, bad things can happen to good investigators. Take steps to protect yourself, and follow outlined safety procedures. The Syfy Channel's *Ghost Hunters* are known for a phrase that pretty well sums it up: "When in doubt, get the hell out!"

12. What Are Ghosts Made Of?

A recent theory is that ghosts are composed of so-called quantum matter, a form of plasma energy that would appear to the observer to exist for only a few seconds at a time. According to this theory, ghosts actually blink in and out of the range of our perceptions continually. Paranormal researcher Paul F. Eno theorizes that ghosts use electromagnetic fields, including those around the human body, to gain access to create a brief tactile sensation. This is how ghosts are able to touch people even though they have no bodies. Previous to this, ghosts were thought to materialize using ectoplasm.

The whole concept of ectoplasm began in 1894, when French physiologist Charles Richet, a winner of the Nobel Prize for Physiology or Medicine in 1913, coined the term to describe the misty substance associated with the formation of ghosts and believed to be the actual physical substance created by the energy manifested by mediums. This rubbery, milky substance could appear either as a solid or a vapor. Extruded from the body of the medium, it would subsequently materialize limbs, faces, and even entire bodies. These manifestations were reportedly warm, flexible, and even doughlike. They emerged from orifices such as the mouth, ears, nose, and occasionally less convenient locations. Forms of ectoplasm varied wildly— anything from mists to thin tentacles to full bodies. This substance disappeared when exposed to light and snapped back quickly into the medium's body. It was believed that touching the ectoplasm or exposing it to light might cause injury to the medium. As any attempt to touch or approach the medium or ectoplasm could cause severe bodily harm, mediums insisted séances take place in almost total darkness.

The fact that these ectoplasmic manifestations occurred in semidarkness and that some were obvious frauds has cast a very negative pall over the whole ectoplasm issue. Of the hundreds of shots of ectoplasm in existence, about 95 percent are less than convincing.

One of the best examples of alleged ectoplasmic mists is from a video shot at the battlefield in Gettysburg, Pennsylvania, posted online in spring of 2007. In it, a DVR recorded what appear to be spirits on the battlefield. It can be viewed at *www.disclose.tv/action/viewvideo/672/Gettysburg_Ghosts*.

13. Do My Eyes Deceive Me?

Occasionally, cameras capture spectral mists and fogs during the course of an investigation. Experienced ghost hunters know these mysterious mists are often the fog caused by exhaled breath on a cold day or a shot of someone's cigarette smoke. Since no one should be smoking during an investigation, hopefully the latter can be ruled out as the cause of the fog during a professional investigation. For the most part, when these eerie mists appear in photos, they were not visible to the naked eye when the pictures were snapped.

So what are we seeing? By following good paranormal investigative protocol, you will perhaps have enough other evidence to help understand what has transpired if such a picture shows up during one of your investigations.

Do you have a record of the room temperature at the time the photo was taken or EMF or infrared DVR readings? If the ambient temperature in the room remained constant but you encountered cold spots or sudden temperature drops, then there is an increased likelihood that something paranormal has been captured in your photos. If you have no other supporting evidence, whether such anomalous images represent genuine ghosts or anything paranormal will very likely be in dispute.

In metaphysical photography, shots that show fogs, mists, and odd-looking lights are often intriguing. In these cloudy shots, it is nearly impossible to tell what the vapor and mists represent.

Paranormal investigators have widely differing opinions regarding orbs, which are odd-looking lights. Some insist that orbs are nothing more than a side effect of the flash going off too close to the lens and bouncing off dust, bugs, or other particles in the air, such as raindrops. Others counter that they can indeed be evidence of paranormal activity or even entities themselves.

Perhaps some can be dismissed as ordinary light pollution, reflections, or cigarette smoke, but when all these things have been eliminated, an impressive number of cloudy images and foggy forms remain. The fact that they seem to happen more frequently in allegedly haunted houses and sites with some religious or spiritual significance is a pertinent observation.

14. Where and What?

The highest concentrations of ghosts and paranormal activity can be found in places where there has been a great deal of human suffering and pain, trauma, or any other strong emotion, such as fear or desperation. Surprisingly, cemeteries aren't that high on the list, but prisons, sanitariums, and hospitals are. Although ghosts can manifest anywhere, they appear most often at night in isolated areas because they cannot manifest around many people. The energy required to materialize physically may be more quickly depleted when one is in contact with the bioelectric fields of other people.

The observed effect of paranormal entities seems to increase in close proximity to water. There are different theories about why this is true, but it has been observed repeatedly. Haunted sites are often near running streams. Occultist Dion Fortune suggested in 1936 that many haunted sites could be attributed to having "ley lines," geomagnetic lines passing through them. Other scientists theorized that ley lines followed lines of energy running throughout Earth and could be detected using dowsing rods.

Ghosts and spirits may communicate through symbolic language, by moving certain objects that have meaning for the percipient—that is, the person perceiving the ghost. Ghosts often make use of a physical environment to draw attention to themselves—changing the temperature of a room or rapping on a wall. Unusual cold spots can be detected and measured by digital thermometers and thermal imagers. When a cold spot is detected, unusual or anomalous phenomena usually follow, such as electronic voice phenomena (EVP), unexplained sounds, unexplained movements of objects, or a sudden feeling of apprehension in witnesses, who may also experience a ghostly touch.

Communication isn't necessarily limited to audio or visual elements. Smells are often associated with hauntings and spirit manifestations. Odors associated with cooking, flowers, tobacco, perfume, the ocean, and even decomposing flesh have been reported at various haunted sites. A haunted house in Wisconsin allegedly produced a smell so foul that it drove away investigators and made the dog they had brought along violently ill.

15. Residual Hauntings

If the same apparition is seen over and over again, doing exactly the same thing, if the same sounds are heard at the same time of day, if the same scene plays out over and over again over a period of years or even centuries, it is a residual haunting. Also called *energy remnants* and *memory imprint*, the apparition in a residual haunting never interacts with onlookers; rather, they seem totally oblivious to them.

Perhaps residual hauntings are simply playbacks of past events. The apparitions involved may not even be actual spirits but just impressions or recordings of events that were so traumatic that they have become imprinted on the very materials of the space in which they occurred. When several different witnesses report seeing the same repetitive event, you can be fairly sure they are reporting an energy remnant from another time.

There are many theories regarding residual hauntings. One of the first to offer a possible hypothesis of how residual hauntings occur was Thomas Charles Lethbridge, in his 1961 book *Ghost and Ghoul.*

His theory is that just as audiotapes and videotapes record sounds and images, certain materials used in the construction of older structures may record impressions of events. If a traumatic, emotionally charged incident occurs, these materials record it for future playback. In this theory, older structures, which often have quartz, iron, and slate in them, are thought to hold an impression of the event. Europe has many ancient structures made of porous stones, which might function like batteries to store energy. This could explain why there are so many instances of haunted sites in Europe. How then do we explain the many residual hauntings in America? Indeed, many of these take place in old buildings as well. New England, as the oldest settled region in the country, seems to be particularly prone to hauntings.

Sometimes there is no visual component to the event, only repetitive sounds, such as footsteps, breathing, or smells that have no apparent cause. No one knows what triggers the playback of these recordings. It could be anything from the observer's own emotional state or sensitivity to weather conditions, such as high humidity or barometric pressure.

Whatever its cause, the residual haunting is intriguing. In the Tower of London, people have seen the ghosts of Anne Boleyn and many others held within its walls before execution.

RESIDUAL HAUNTINGS AT GETTYSBURG

Battlefields where many fought and died, often in agony, are the perfect settings for residual hauntings. Gettysburg, Pennsylvania, was the scene of a horrific battle during the U.S. Civil War. On the battlefield, observers have seen ghosts of soldiers charging downhill. They have heard troops singing Irish folksongs and the sounds of battle—swords clanging, thundering hoofbeats, the cries of the dying.

Devil's Den, the site of heavy fighting on the second day of battle, July 2, 1863, is a prime location for a residual haunting. Even before the three-day battle that took place there, the site had earned its name from reports of paranormal activity. After the battle and up to the present day, visitors have reported seeing an apparition that may be the ghost of a Texas infantryman, sometimes gesturing or motioning but never speaking or interacting with onlookers. Some say he is the ghost of a sniper who held the Northern troops at bay on Little Round Top.

16. Intelligent and Human Hauntings

Ghosts who have not yet crossed over, have unfinished business, or are too emotionally attached to a person or place and can't move on are classified as intelligent human hauntings. They linger for a reason; they are trying to get your attention. These entities can interact with humans, and sometimes do so in a spectacular fashion.

Signs of an Intelligent Haunting

- Objects disappear then reappear in impossible places
- Cold spots and the strong sense of a presence or someone watching
- Strange, unexplained sounds
- Furniture and small objects move by themselves—and are sometimes even thrown
- Doors and windows open and close inexplicably
- Lights, televisions, radios, and faucets turn on and off on their own

These apparitions have a mission to complete and they are looking for assistance—possibly, your assistance. If the ghost is interactive and trying to communicate, it is most definitely an intelligent human haunting. Sometimes this sort of haunting occurs shortly after a friend or loved one dies. It is as if he is trying to comfort or communicate with those left behind. When an entity is strongly attached to a specific site, person, or object, he may try to protect it. This is a very common occurrence; after all, when a person dies, he may not even realize it. If he has lived in a house for many years, he may refuse to leave it even after he has passed on. He may think the new residents are trespassers and may quite naturally try to scare them into leaving.

In intelligent hauntings, the entity retains the personality and appearance of the deceased person or animal. Sometimes, strangely, they even appear wearing the same clothing they were wearing before passing over.

The ghosts of animals, particularly pets, are sometimes reported. Spirit cats are the most common. Animals that become attached to a location or person can also be interactive, and thus termed intelligent hauntings.

How can you tell an intelligent haunting from more general paranormal activity? Talk to the witnesses. Listen carefully and take notes. The witnesses' reports of what has transpired will quickly determine whether you are dealing with a residual haunting or an intelligent one.

Intelligent hauntings without a human component have also been documented. These types of hauntings are poltergeists. They are not human, but they still seem to have an agenda they wish to accomplish, and they are most definitely interactive—in fact, most of the time too much so.

Part 3

IN THE FIELD: PRACTICAL SKILLS AND WORK ON LOCATION

If fools rush in where angels fear to tread, what shall we call the ghost hunter who does the same? All kidding aside, proper preparation makes a great difference in your experience of investigating the paranormal. To get the most out of it, you must put your best into all the various phases. Your priorities should be to ensure that proper procedures and protocols are in place before beginning the investigation and to maintain a professional demeanor when interacting with the client.

17. An Investigator's Common Sense Checklist

Kym Black, a sensitive who works with The Rhode Island Paranormal Research Group (T.R.I.P.R.G.), notes that before an investigation starts, the investigators run through a mental checklist of dos and don'ts:

+ *Tie back long hair.* Hair that is not tied back can move in front of the lens and produce what appears to be an anomaly. In these shots, the hair strands can actually look like a ghostly blur. Light hair is particularly troublesome; it doesn't block the light as much and the flash burns out all detail. The same is true of wrist straps on cameras. Part of the strap can whip in front of the lens, causing inexperienced photographers/investigators to think they have captured a paranormal shot.
+ *No smoking.* Obviously, smoking on an investigation can make analyzing evidence of ghostly fogs very tricky.
+ *Double check all equipment beforehand to be sure it is working properly.* Batteries in cameras, flashlights, DVRs, and scanners should be fully charged. Keep replacements on hand. Also, make sure you have gloves, boots, odor-free insect repellant, an analog wristwatch, and a notebook and pencil.
+ *Make sure you have all safety equipment*: walkie-talkies and/or cell phones, a first-aid kit, and perhaps most importantly, an alternative light source such as a kerosene lantern or candles and matches.

18. Doing a Walk-Through and Site Check with the Client

Once an investigation starts, the case manger should meet with the client and take an exploratory walk-through of the site. This is a good time to set up the option to return after the investigation, if necessary; follow-ups are often needed to recheck data or gather more evidence after the initial analysis. If the client has any special requests or has recent activity to report, this is her chance to share the information.

The walk-through provides an opportunity for the investigator to take baseline readings with monitoring equipment. Ideally, this meeting should be done a bit in advance of the investigation so the information can be coordinated and possibly researched more deeply. It isn't always possible to do a walk-through before the day of the investigation, especially if the site is far away or time is tight.

If possible, walk through the investigation site in daylight, when anything that may be a physical hazard can be identified. Older and abandoned buildings are interesting to investigate and often have unexplained phenomena associated with them, but they can have many lurking hazards as well.

Ask plenty of questions. You are in the business of seeking answers, so practice asking questions without being too intrusive. Ask about common hazards, including:

+ Structurally unsound areas—weak floors, uneven floors with loose boards, unsafe steps or balconies
+ Clutter and debris

- Areas or rooms where hazardous chemicals are stored
- Rooms under construction where nails or sharp-edged tools can be found
- Rooms containing asbestos insulation or other dangerous materials

Other impediments to an investigation could be:

- Antiques and collectibles that cannot be touched or moved
- Areas with high EMF readings
- Areas to which the client refuses access

All pertinent information about the building or site should be noted. Determine the age of the site. The current owner may not know, but a records search will uncover the site's age and ownership history. Never take a building's appearance as a sure indicator of its age; it could have been remodeled and may look far younger than it is or could be cleverly designed to look like an old structure although it was built only a few years ago. New buildings do seem to have less ghostly activity than old ones, so knowing the age may help you gauge whether the reports you are hearing are credible.

If you have been told the history of the site, do your own independent verification of the facts. Misinformation and faulty memories cloud the data quite often, so double check everything you can. Always check at the local city or town hall for ownership records and building permits. You may be able to check these records online. You can also do a bit of genealogy research at *www.ancestry.com* and *www.familysearch.org*.

Links to other genealogy sites can be found at *www.cyndislist* *.com*.

CREATING AN ENVIRONMENTAL WORKSHEET

Jeff Barnes is a ghost hunter in Indiana *(http://poseyghosts* *.wordpress.com)*. In one of his podcasts, he talks about putting together an environmental worksheet for your investigation. This worksheet lists conditions in the home that might adversely impact the client's home and health and even the investigation. He recommends looking for wiring issues, mold, air quality, and leaks. None of these problems are unique to paranormal investigation procedures, but knowing about them may help you document circumstances that might support or debunk the perception of paranormal activity at an investigation site. Perhaps your client is seeing things because toxic paint fumes are poisoning the air.

Structural issues such as cracks in the floors or walls should also be noted, as should basements with bare earth floors, which might be contaminated with industrial waste. Faulty electrical wiring can cause high EMF readings, which in turn can cause paranoia in sensitive people. Mold and plumbing problems like malfunctioning hidden drains can contribute to the accumulation of sewer gas, which can definitely affect the client's behavior.

If anything looks as if it is going to cause a problem for the team, make a note of it and/or take a picture of it. This way the team can be fully briefed about any potentially dangerous areas or situations before they get to the site. They should also be alerted if a spot will be virtually impossible to investigate due to high EMF readings or other natural barriers or obstacles.

The walk-through is an opportunity to get important information from the client. The client should point out areas of particular concern or where something unusual has been seen, heard, or smelled. Sometimes people remember facts or concerns they forgot to mention initially, and walking around the property jogs their memory.

19. Equipment Check and Deployment

Ideally, there should be one person in charge of the equipment. In most professional organizations, an equipment manager charges and tests the batteries, checks out and packs up the equipment before the investigation, deploys the equipment on site, then breaks everything down and packs it up neatly and safely at the end of the night for the return trip to headquarters.

Investigators are so exhausted at the end of a hunt that it is always tempting to cut corners when packing the equipment away. Whoever does it is in charge of a lot of expensive gear, so be sure that your group designates a responsible volunteer.

Some amateur groups do not have a lot of equipment, and the equipment they do have is owned by the individual team members. In these cases, everyone is in charge of their own equipment.

The equipment manager should also be in charge of evaluating how much equipment to bring along on the investigation. Bringing too much gear increases set-up time and is harder to monitor. Each case requires different equipment and a different setup. The theory is, the more gear at the investigation, the more likely it is to capture evidence. However, don't bring superfluous equipment.

Small homes or sites require a very streamlined approach. Remember, if five cameras are running, there will be five hours of tape to review for each hour of the investigation. Novice investigators may have less equipment, but they also have a shorter setup and breakdown time. Luggage with wheels is great for hauling equipment into and out of the site, and is also a great solution for transport and storage problems.

20. Recording Data and Observations Manually

Keeping track of data is important, and data logs play a vital role in an investigation. The team leader understands this; in an efficiently run organization, so do the other team members.

If a member consistently keeps poor records or doesn't turn in records at all, her contribution to the team is going to be compromised. New members should undergo comprehensive training and a probationary period during which they learn the technological side of ghost hunting; keeping track of data and other records should be included in this training.

Modern ghost hunters adhere to the scientific method, so learning correct methodology is critical. Here is the correct record-keeping methodology in a nutshell:

+ Take baseline readings.
+ Record the date, time, and place.
+ Note the site location, client name, and client contact information.
+ Record the environmental conditions such as moon phase, outside temperature, inside temperature, humidity, wind speed, weather, and barometric pressure.
+ Record initial impressions and comments.
+ Use an equipment list.
+ List investigators involved.
+ Record client data and interviews.

21. Client Interviews and Collecting Eyewitness Accounts

Are you a good listener? Do you have an easy rapport with people, an empathic and sympathetic nature? If so, you are in luck. These skills are in demand for ghost hunters. A very important part of the process is talking to eyewitnesses and gathering as much information as possible about the haunting.

People who are dealing with a poltergeist or haunting will often be in a highly stressed state. They may feel as if they are going crazy or that they will be labeled as unstable or worse if they disclose what they have seen. They often fear ridicule and want to feel that their anonymity will be protected.

Independent investigators should deal with clients as though they are interviewing witnesses to an accident. Although many levelheaded people claim to have seen ghosts, you should rule out all other possibilities and find out exactly what they saw or heard, while maintaining your own sense of professionalism.

It is vital to interview potential clients and witnesses before committing to an investigation. They are the ones with the inside information and they will usually initiate the contact with the investigators. It's your duty to properly assess the request.

- Is the client believable and not a hoaxster? A personal interview can help you determine the answer to this. Ask yourself if you have a gut feeling about the client, and trust it. Does she make you feel uneasy, or try to frighten or intimidate you?
- Is the client mentally stable and not under treatment for a psychiatric disorder or substance abuse problems?
- Is the situation the client describes a dangerous one that needs immediate attention?

The answers to these questions are almost impossible to determine with just a phone call. Someone from the group must interview the client in person. Although people may balk at answering personal questions, filling out a form can be a little less threatening. The interviewer can look the completed form over and ask follow-up questions. The form is an icebreaker, and it provides a permanent record of the initial meeting. Facts pertinent to the case can be readily available to the team as they conduct the investigation. This form should include the date and case number, the location, the name of the person being interviewed, and a description of the phenomena the client has observed.

A client's privacy *must* be respected if she chooses to remain anonymous, and team members should be discreet when making any sort of reference to the investigation. The client's identity, address, and phone number should never be given out without her express written permission. The last thing people want is for their location or name to be disclosed.

Part of a psychic investigator's job is reassuring clients that their experiences are not unique. This is where your extensive reading on the paranormal and self-education in all things supernatural can be extremely helpful. You must also project an air of professionalism that reassures clients the investigation is in good hands and will be conducted with the proper professionalism and competency. The last thing in the world the victim of a haunting needs is to feel jeopardized by the investigation. Clients are owed respect, for themselves and their property. Particular care must be taken in households with children. Don't scare them or talk too much about the investigation in their presence.

22. Confidentiality and Protecting the Client's Privacy

The client who has reached a decision to contact a paranormal investigator or a team of ghost hunters is very likely a person who has undergone very unusual or even inexplicable experiences. Very often, clients feel as if they may be losing their grip on reality. They may have been ridiculed if they mentioned that something supernatural was taking place around them.

When a client finds you, he may be emotionally vulnerable. It is part of your job to reassure him that you will do everything in your power to safeguard his privacy. You must also assure him that while an investigation is taking place at his home or business, the people who are involved in that investigation will protect and respect his property, treat it with consideration, and, most importantly, let the client retain his anonymity, should he want it—most do.

What does client confidentiality mean, in practical terms? Many groups and investigators approach it differently, but to most, it means:

+ The identity of the client and the client's family are not disclosed.
+ The location of the investigation is kept secret, especially in a small town.
+ Facts about the case that could eventually lead to the deduction of the identity of the site or the person(s) are suppressed.

This means training investigators to watch their tongues when talking about their activities. Several pieces of information casually sprinkled though a conversation that can lead someone to deduce the client's identity or reach a conclusion about the site's location is the most common form of slipup. People mean no harm, but it is very unprofessional and may result in actual legal liability if the client can prove he was damaged as a result.

Most teams sign a confidentiality agreement to reassure clients their information will be kept confidential. The documents vary in length and complexity, but all have one thing in common: they warrant that information gathered in the course of the investigation is treated as privileged and private. All team members should read it and sign it, to reinforce the idea that responsibility and liability to the client are on the shoulders of the investigators.

A bare-bones agreement should contain the following information:

CONFIDENTIALITY AGREEMENT FORM

We respect your privacy rights. We guarantee that your confidential information will remain so. We treat as confidential any information divulged during the course of the investigation, as well as any information that may be inadvertently obtained during the course of the investigation. These facts include the names and identities of all parties, clients, and witnesses, as well as the physical address of the investigation or any other feature that may make the site readily identifiable.

On occasion, this organization may ask to use information and evidence collected during the investigation for educational or publicity purposes, or possibly for inclusion on our website. Please check the level of confidentiality you would like to request and with which you would feel comfortable.

_____Full disclosure, including the identity of witnesses, clients, and the site location

_____ Partial disclosure, including the identity of witnesses and clients, but the site location is changed and the exact address of the location is undisclosed

_____No disclosure of any of the pertinent facts of the case whatsoever

SPECIAL REQUESTS

_____

_____

_____

_____

Signed _____
Date_____

There are those rare times when investigators are not required to conceal information about the case. These usually arise in instances where the allegedly haunted site would actually benefit from the notoriety the investigation would bring, such as the Lizzie Borden Bed and Breakfast in Fall River, Massachusetts, which has only benefited from the exposure it has received from being featured on *Ghost Hunters.*

These cases are a delightful breath of fresh air to investigators. They can free the group to break loose from the constraints of confidentiality and discuss the case with other paranormal investigators. The nonconfidential cases allow the ghost hunters to freely discuss their fascinating experiences and dissect the phenomena with other groups. It also gives the team a chance to post its findings about the case, along with EVPs, photos, and other evidence, online.

23. Educating and Comforting Clients

In investigating self-generated cases, such as reports of apparitions seen along the roadside, paranormal investigators have the luxury of being able to put the investigation first, as there are no clients to deal with. They may proceed with the ghost hunt without having to consider the impact the investigation may have on their clients, so they can experiment with new equipment and techniques. But this sort of investigation happens rarely; most often the team will be called in to investigate when there is paranormal activity that is affecting people's lives.

Sadly, sometimes investigators who embark on challenging cases are so wrapped up in the thrill of the hunt that they forget the human aspects of the job. If an investigative team is called in to discover the reasons behind paranormal activity, it is usually because truly disturbing or threatening events have disrupted the lives of the clients. Although every client will be different, one constant seems to be that the situation will have reached a stage that is disturbing to the people in the environment. Paranormal investigator Nathan Schoonover asserts, "With me, it is never about the proof. It is about helping people." Schoonover primarily consults on cases of malign hauntings.

Even if the clients seem to be maintaining their composure, they may be putting up a brave front for the investigators. A good approach to take is to reassure the person that she has made the right decision to call the team in. Act as professionally and calmly as possible during the execution of the interview and investigation. This is reassuring to the client, and that is particularly necessary if she seems to be at the physical or mental breaking point.

Clients who appear extremely agitated or on the verge of a mental breakdown should always be referred immediately to a health care professional.

If the haunting is making the client frightened or even just uncomfortable, she may opt to seek a way of ridding the premises of the supernatural pests. Part of your responsibility as a paranormal investigator is to try to find a means of bringing closure to this sort of client, either through your own team's efforts or through the help of outside experts in cleansing and closure. In extreme cases, exorcism may be warranted. If the entities can be convinced to leave the premises and cross over into the light, the outcome is optimal for everyone involved.

Never say or do anything to alarm or frighten your client. Be sensitive to your client's frame of mind. Strive to soothe and calm the situation and educate the client as to what is happening without making the situation worse than it is.

24. Making an Honest Assessment: Is It Worth Investigating?

First, you need to determine what is actually happening. An honest assessment of the situation, phenomenon, activity, and people involved may not always support further investigation. Are there ever times when a case is dropped after the preliminary interview? Absolutely. Seasoned investigators realize that it is a big drain on resources to pursue a case when there is little likelihood that the disturbance is paranormal. They also will not continue an investigation if:

1. There is obviously a natural explanation for what is occurring
2. It is apparent the investigators are being lied to or set up
3. The situation is in a state of flux, and the malevolent energy present actually requires the services of a demonologist
4. One of the parties involved objects to the investigation

25. Integrity and Accountability to Clients

The client has invited you into his home and trusted you with access to the minutiae of his day-to-day life. He is virtually at the mercy of the team who is conducting the investigation, not only in terms of his privacy but also in respect to property damage and misappropriation. Every attempt should be made not to violate his trust in any way.

Case files should be locked and inaccessible to anyone but authorized team members. Confidentiality agreements should be reviewed before public relations work or media interviews. If case files are no longer needed, they should be shredded.

REQUIREMENTS FOR MAINTAINING PROFESSIONALISM AND OBJECTIVITY

+ Careful record keeping
+ A sense of responsibility to both the client and the team
+ Never fudging data or attempting to support bad data by suppressing evidence
+ Discarding any evidence that could be explained by natural means
+ Careful coordination of experiential and technical data
+ Reviewing the rules of conduct

INVESTIGATION RULES OF CONDUCT

Every organization should have a brief list of rules of conduct, which should be reviewed as a reminder before any investigation. Make the language plain and unequivocal. Suit it to the needs of your team, and be sure they have all read and agreed to it before the investigation starts.

INVESTIGATION DOS AND DON'TS

+ Do address the client by name in a respectful manner when introduced. Make eye contact. Shake hands.
+ Do listen to any special requests or concerns the client mentions. Honor them.
+ Do maintain a pleasant, professional demeanor.
+ Do respect private property and the client's personal belongings.
+ Do tie back long hair.
+ Do bring along a signed form granting permission to investigate.
+ Don't smoke in the area being investigated.
+ Don't drink alcohol or use drugs before or during an investigation.
+ Don't wear perfume, cologne, or after-shave.
+ Don't be disrespectful in any way to the client or contradict her as she relates her experiences.
+ Don't interfere with personal belongings or open drawers in private areas of the home, such as bedrooms.

- Don't comment about the condition of the premises, particularly if they are messy or in disrepair.
- Don't remove anything from the site without express permission of the client.

Members should be briefed on what is expected from them as far as their interactions with clients and the client's property.

As guests in the client's home, they should conduct themselves as such. It isn't good procedure to flip though personal papers, read diaries, poke through drawers or medicine cabinets, or even to make personal comments about the appearance of the premises or clients, unless it has a direct bearing on something pertinent to the case.

Likewise, be respectful when visiting cemeteries to conduct an investigation. Respect the departed, take care not to step on graves or lean on headstones, and speak softly and courteously if you are attempting EVP work. This is just good manners; it also protects investigators from the wrath of territorial ghosts.

26. Showing the Data to the Client

Sometimes known as the reveal, showing the evidence of a haunting (or lack thereof) and the plan for dealing with it is an art unto itself. The client has expectations, and staying professional while you meet those expectations will keep you in the business.

Arrange a meeting time that is convenient for both you and the client. Expect to spend about thirty to sixty minutes on the actual presentation and discussion of the evidence, depending on what you have found. Block out some time after the reveal to answer any questions or concerns the client may have. If you found evidence of a haunting, your suggestions for handling the situation should be discussed with the client at this time. Draw up a plan that everyone agrees to.

The follow-up meeting can be held at your office or at the client's home or office. It should have a space where you can set up a conference-type arrangement, with a table large enough to accommodate several team members and the client(s). Make sure an electrical outlet is nearby if you need it for any of your equipment.

Set up your laptop and evidence files so that everyone can easily see what is happening. Before the reveal, you should load the photos, video, and audio files into the computer. Make a shortcut to the folder; all files should be easily accessible on the desktop. Avoid fumbling through files and trying to locate the evidence as the client watches; it does not send the message that you're professional.

When you meet, ask if any activity has occurred since the investigation. Remind the client that your job is to look for any possible natural causes for what she is experiencing. Tell her if you were able to debunk anything and discuss any personal experiences investigators had while there. Then show or reveal the hard evidence—any photos, EVPs, or videos of anomalous events.

27. Following Up

Some investigators simply establish whether or not there is paranormal activity actually taking place. What the client wishes to do with that information is his own concern.

More frequently, if the team finds evidence that a residence is haunted, they will work with the client to find an outcome for the situation that works for him.

Reactions vary. Some people are delighted to find that their suspicions are true. This is particularly common when the reputation as a haunted location can enhance the owner's commercial interest in a property, say in the case of a haunted hotel or restaurant, which can see a huge boom in business as curiosity seekers flock to the establishment to see what all the fuss is about.

No matter what the outcome of the case, the client's information should be kept on file. Follow up periodically to see how your clients are doing. They really appreciate this, and you must make sure they are still okay, particularly if your team detected evidence of a dark or oppressive presence.

In cases where the client has opted to live with the haunting, check to make sure that nothing has changed for the worse and that he is still comfortable with the situation. Active sites that have an ongoing presence can be a real resource for a paranormal group; if the owner is willing, it can become a site for more in-depth investigations and a training ground for new members.

28. Extended Investigations and Repeat Offenders

It is not unusual to have a case that continues far beyond the scope of a preliminary investigation. If the evidence found during the initial investigation proves promising, the team may return again and again to gather evidence.

A prerequisite, of course, is that the haunting is not causing problems for the client and that he has decided he can live with the situation. When people understand that the ghost is not trying to harm anyone, they often accept the situation and decide to peacefully coexist. This allows investigators the opportunity to delve deeper into the case and gather more evidence.

Some cases are so active that the team can barely scratch the surface in just one visit, and it may be possible to do an investigation that stretches out over the course of days. If the site is secure, the investigators have the added advantage of leaving the equipment set up and in place.

Another reason to follow up on a case is when the entity that was bothering the client has returned. When this happens, the team has to return to the site and try to evaluate the situation. Is it really the site that is haunted, or is it the people? This has to be determined first and may take a great deal of work to uncover. Sometimes it is clear that the client has personal issues that are far graver than dealing with a few ectoplasmic entities.

If a client believes she has been the victim of a demonic oppression, she may be emotionally and physically exhausted, and should be referred for appropriate follow-up treatment by mental health practitioners. Investigations can continue while this is going on, but you should exercise extreme caution and consult with a demonologist or person who deals with malevolent entities regularly.

Some of the most spectacular evidence of paranormal activity has been witnessed during this type of case, but the well-being of the client and the safety of your team should always take precedence over evidence gathering.

Sometimes the team may return to a site that was promising at first but that produced no hard evidence. If a team refuses to use any sort of psychic or sensitive or even an investigator's own personal experience to document paranormal activity, they will need to return to gather evidence that can be verified through technological documentation. Although some think modern ghost hunting relies too much on science and prefer the experiences of sensitives and psychics, many groups now stick to the hard-evidence protocols.

During a long investigation, you may find it helpful to use additional instruments to gather hard evidence, such as mobile weather stations, which record data such as humidity and air movement. They can also identify potentially ordinary explanations for reports of activity, such as drafty windows and old radiators.

29. The Client's Responsibility

A lot has been said about the paranormal organization's responsibilities to the client and to its own team members, but we must remember that the client has responsibilities, too. When a client calls an organization to investigate unexplained phenomena in her home, there is usually no charge for the service and the investigators bear the brunt of the expenses.

The client should keep this in mind when requesting help. She should be as cooperative and helpful as possible. What should the client do?

1. Be truthful about the phenomena she has been experiencing. This means no exaggerations, equivocations, or withholding of evidence.
2. Allow the investigators full access to areas where activities have occurred.
3. Try not to place too many restrictions if full access can't be granted.
4. Be courteous and hospitable.

30. Remaining Objective and Professional

Perhaps the biggest challenge that novice ghost hunters face is remaining objective about the phenomena they are called in to observe. You should try to bring as much professionalism and objectivity as you can in your evidence gathering.

Ghost hunters who conclude that most of the sites they investigate are haunted are doing something seriously wrong. Professional investigators say that only 10 percent of their cases show any evidence of paranormal activity; others assert that even that number is too high.

Whether or not the team doing the investigation witnesses an apparition, the anxiety and expectations of the clients at a haunted site can sometimes trigger another sort of observer effect. These effects can be a combination of misperceptions and misidentifications of ordinary events. Eagerness to witness paranormal activity can set other activities in motion, quite literally. Unusual physical activity observed on-site may actually be a result of psychokinesis (PK), the power of the human mind to move matter. In this case, the events are very hard to classify. You could be dealing with a real haunting or just an instance of PK not caused by the originating phenomenon.

Part 4

ANALYSIS AND REVIEW
OF EVIDENCE

What is real? How do you know if you've encountered a ghost? First, rule out all other explainable phenomena. Always remember that what is experienced as "real" in any haunting may be taking place only in the minds of the onlookers. The human mind has a tendency to create situations that seem paranormal, so a rational approach is the best tool in determining if the sources of the events truly are paranormal.

Sometimes there's a rational explanation for something that appears to be paranormal. For example, infrasound is low-frequency sound, and although audible to the human ear, it may not register on a conscious level. Small motors produce these sound waves, which resonate around eighteen or nineteen cycles per second. The human eyeball has a resonance frequency of eighteen cycles a second, so the theory goes that the sound wave produced by the motor sets up a sympathetic resonance in the eye, triggering the impression of fleeting images. It can sometimes cause people to believe they are seeing things out of the corners of their eyes, or to experience the creepy sensation of being watched.

31. Evaluating the Evidence

After the team members complete their various inquiries and feel it is time to evaluate the evidence, they will wrap up the investigation for the night and remove their people and equipment. The photos, taped footage, and audiotapes must all be reviewed by team members and thoroughly sifted for any possible paranormal activity. This is a very time-consuming process.

The team members' activity logs and notes on personal experiences are also thoroughly reviewed, and the lead investigators may use all the information from the investigation to draw conclusions about possible natural explanations. A local group with the option of returning to the site to gather more data may decide if it is warranted. If a conclusion can be drawn based on the evidence, the investigators set up a meeting with the client to reveal the results of the investigation. At the meeting, they show all the evidence that supports the haunting. If there is none, they reveal that, too.

If there is clear evidence of a haunting, the investigators state what sort of situation they feel the client is facing. They will then offer their professional recommendations for dealing with it. This can range from advising the client to ignore the activity to calling in sensitives to clear the space of any negative energy. This phase often requires educating clients about the threat level and the various sorts of hauntings. Clients are often relieved that their claims have been validated and feel that they can live with the spirits, as long as they are benign.

Sometimes clients are very disappointed if nothing has been found.

32. Hard Evidence Versus Personal Experiences

Personal experiences that are not independently verifiable by written or recorded means are just that—merely personal experiences, not hard evidence. In order to obtain evidence about something that is so hard to quantify, investigators have to come up with procedures and methods that ensure something virtually unquantifiable is quantified—a tall order, indeed.

Ghost hunter Loyd Auerbach feels that the careful use of the tools modern science has given us can help paranormal investigators gather hard evidence. One such tool is the use of sidereal time instead of solar time. This way of measuring time is determined by looking at the position of particular stars and constellations overhead. Since the sidereal day is a few minutes shorter than a solar day, there are windows that are said to allow people to be more psychically active. If this theory is true, investigators may be able to use these LST (local sidereal time) windows in their quest to obtain more verifiable data about ghosts and hauntings by scheduling investigations during those windows, or by paying closer attention to data collected during those times.

At *http://tycho.usno.navy.mil/sidereal.html*, you can find the exact sidereal time for your location if you know the longitude.

You can determine your latitude by going to *http://geocoder.us* and inputting an address.

33. Analyzing the Evidence

Wouldn't you think this would be the fun part? Well, no, not usually. Those in the field who regularly review evidence from an investigation must have a very high tolerance for boredom. After all, they may have to spend hours reviewing audio, still photos, video, thermal images, digital thermometer readings, and the team's logbooks. Only very rarely do they actually pick up something noteworthy.

In most groups, more than one person is assigned to do evidence-review duty. Having two people doing evidence review is the best approach. Not only does it go twice as fast, but when one person finds an anomaly, the other can verify if it is actually a significant find or debunk it if it is not.

The evidence gathered on scene is placed together in one location, ideally a table large enough to set up the computers, monitors, camcorders, and other equipment. The people who will be reviewing the evidence sit side by side, with headphones on so as not to disturb one another. When something is found, say an EVP, the investigator who discovered it will ask a fellow investigator to take a look or listen to the anomaly. This is the fun part, and it's the payoff to slogging through the many uneventful hours of evidence review.

When something is discovered, the time and place are noted and cross-indexed with the other tapes, photos, and notes to see if there may be some correlation or backup verification on them as well. The team's energy level soars if this happens; it is the reward for all their hard work.

The evidence is then copied and archived to be reviewed later by the whole team, which may validate or debunk it. Only credible evidence is presented to the client at the reveal.

34. What to Look For

What do evidence reviewers watch for in photos, videotapes, and thermal images? Anything that is out of the ordinary, but most particularly such things as doors or objects moving with no one in the area; shadows, mists, and fogs forming under strange circumstances; lights or orbs moving through a scene; apparitions; and bizarre temperature anomalies. These are all immediate red flags that something paranormal is happening.

If anything of this sort is captured, the reviewers ask for assistance in assessing what they have found. Then the inves·tigators try to think of any possible reasons to debunk the evidence. For example, investigators might ask themselves whether it was possible for the door to open because there was a strong wind whipping through the house. They would then be obliged to check other data against that suspicion, searching the logs to see if other investigators noted that the wind had picked up at that point. They would also check to see if cameras in other parts of the house had detected something similar occurring at that exact instant. Evidence is always correlated and crosschecked. If there is a possible natural explanation, the evidence has to be thrown out.

35. Being Aware of Matrixing Anomalies

People often perceive random images as having significance. Matrixing refers to the human mind's ability to take random sensory data and rearrange it so that it forms a recognizable and familiar image or sound. It is what we do when we gaze up at clouds in the sky and find a resemblance in them to a face, an animal, or any other familiar image. This natural tendency is just a mental filling in of the blanks. Matrixing can be useful. It allows us to interpret data quickly and organize it into coherent messages. It also lets us distinguish subtle nuances in similar patterns.

In other cases, it may not be useful, but it's harmless. We've all heard of the cinnamon bun that looks like Mother Teresa or the water stain on a wall that resembles Jesus.

However, if matrixing makes us see things that aren't there during a paranormal investigation, that creates a problem. When we see the image of a face leering out from the wallpaper, sometimes it is merely a chance resemblance, with no basis in or relationship to actuality. These images are called matrixing anomalies.

Paranormal investigators must be very careful not to fall victim to matrixing anomalies. The images or sounds they see and record must be analyzed objectively, as the human mind always wants to make order out of chaos.

The biggest problem for paranormal researchers concerns matrixing anomalies that happen during the evidence reviews, when someone spots an image or sound that appears to indicate paranormal activity. Careful review by several individuals is sometimes necessary to disprove that the image is of supernatural origin. Remember, whenever a natural explanation for a phenomenon is found, the paranormal explanation is thrown out.

Grant Wilson of The Atlantic Paranormal Society (TAPS) has spoken and written about matrixing anomalies. The following guidelines for investigators are based on his information:

1. Is the photo you're analyzing mostly trees, fields, cluttered areas, or reflective surfaces, such as mirrors and glass? If the image is made up of complex shapes and patterns, there is plenty of raw material for the mind to use in fabricating images, such as a face or silhouette.

2. Zero in on the face or figure. Is it made up of its own unique material or of the components of the picture? If it is truly paranormal, the face or figure should be made up of its own separate materials, not the material that comprises the rest of the image. Take the example of a face in the forest. If it is made up of branches and leaves, it is matrixing. If not, you may have something truly paranormal.

3. If you are satisfied that the two previous criteria have been met, closely examine the anomaly. If it is a face or figure, are the proportions correct or are they disproportionate? If the proportions are distorted, that

is a problem—the image you have found is probably naturally occurring.

Matrixing can occur with sound as well as video. As soon as a sound is identified as being anomalous, it must be played over and over again until the listener is eventually able to discern what is being said. If you have to listen to a sound clip dozens of times, artificially boost it a great deal, or play it backward, you are probably dealing with a naturally occurring sound.

36. Reviewing Photos and Video

People are often better at catching one sort of evidence than another. Maggie Florio, an investigator with The Rhode Island Paranormal Research Group (T.R.I.P.R.G.) is excellent at capturing EVPs, and Kym Black, also with T.R.I.P.R.G., is great at capturing photos of anomalies, mists, and orbs. Not only are they better at capturing their specific phenomena, they are also better at detecting it during the evidence review.

To effectively review video and photo evidence, you'll need the following characteristics:

+ Patience
+ Good vision

+ Awareness of matrixing
+ Experience

Videotape the client as he reports the phenomenon so that investigators can review it later. Sometimes the investigator's recollection of what the client reported is wrong, which can lead to incorrect conclusions.

On Episode 63 of *Ghost Hunters*, TAPS investigated the Ruff Stone Tavern in North Providence, Rhode Island. During the walk-through, the proprietress said that she had experienced a strange scent, like that of a woman, in the bar. Grant asked what sort of scent, and she replied, "Musky." Later, when he was attempting to debunk this, he opened some chemicals and bottles in the vicinity, but they were obviously not the source of the odor. Then he opened a drawer and said he thought he had found the source of the odor; it smelled "musty."

Musty and musky are two very different odors, but the words do sound alike. Musk is a scent used in perfumes; "musty" is used to describe the odor of mildew or mold. The two are very different, but no one appears to have caught the distinction. Investigators can catch this sort of error through the use of video or audiotape.

Almost nothing is more important than paying very strict attention during an evidence review. Few aspects of the case require as much diligence as the evidence-review phase of the investigation. It will not matter if the team has gathered tons of great evidence if the reviewers don't analyze it carefully, noting any discrepancies.

37. Evidence Preservation and Preparation

Photos, videos, and audio recordings (digital and analog), as well as thermal imaging files, are common types of evidence captured in the course of a site investigation. Sometimes these files can be enhanced through the use of specially designed software.

Make sure to follow the two rules of evidence:

+ Always make file backups of the original files on a separate media storage device, CD, DVD, or flash drive. You should have two copies of both the originals and of the enhanced versions.
+ Never alter a file and save over it. Before you do anything to a file, create a copy to work on and leave the original in a pristine state, unaltered. Save digital photo originals as TIFFs. Analog photos should be scanned at 300 dpi, at 100 percent.

Get the evidence in the best possible shape before sharing it with the client. Use an image-processing program to increase contrast and bring out detail on photos, and clean up audio files to remove any distracting static and hissing.

Photoshop Elements is a great program for resizing, cropping, and enhancing the contrast and brightness of digital photos. Proper image enhancement isn't hard to learn and can make a huge difference in the perception of the data. There are programs that can be used to clean up digital video, but many investigators choose to send this out to be done in order to avoid any accusation of manipulating the data.

Audio files can be cleaned up easily enough with programs you can download from the Internet such as WavePad and Audacity. Thermal images usually have high contrast and brightness and do not require any enhancement.

38. CD or DVD Digital Storage

The records, logs, and evidence for each investigation must be keyed and correlated to one another in a master organizational system. In most organizations, as soon as a new case opens, the case manager sets up a file folder for it on the computer and assigns a case number. For example, the first investigation of 2009 could be named 09-001-Ellis. The first two digits denote the year and the middle three refer to the order in which the case was received. (The second case of the year would be 002.) The client's name finishes up the case number. Subfolders should have the case number and the type of files to be found within them, such as 09-001-Ellis-Audio, 09-001-Ellis-Photos, 09-001-Ellis-Video. If more than one investigator did audio or EVP work, it may be necessary to create a subfolder within the audio subfolder with the case number, the subfolder name, and the name of the investigator, such as 09-001-Ellis-Audio-Melissa.

Since much of the evidence gathered during the course of the investigation is digital—audio, video, and photography—it must be carefully stored. Digital media can be lost or misplaced, and it isn't cheap to replace. The evidence or records on the lost media is often irreplaceable.

The individual investigators on a case can handle their stored digital media in one of several ways, each with its pros and cons:

1. Place digital media cards into small baggies tagged with the case number and their names, then hand them over to the team leader. The team leader submits them for evidence review. This option allows the team leader to keep control of the data. Team members may feel more comfortable with this option if the media cards belong to the group and they are not expected to turn over their own property.

2. Investigators upload the digital files to their home computers, where they label it by case number and make a copy of the files for the evidence-review process. In this approach, the individual investigators are responsible for making sure the evidence eventually reaches the group. If they are not well-trained and conscientious investigators, evidence can be accidentally damaged or destroyed.

3. Investigators review the files individually and hand over copies of any files that appear to contain unexplained activity. This approach has the least merit, as it relies on just one investigator to review the evidence, but it can be quite a time saver for the evidence reviewers, removing hours of tedium from their job. This approach works best when the investigators have years of working expe-

rience and the team has completed many investigations together and implicitly trusts each member's judgment.

Whatever approach is used for preserving and reviewing the digital files, the group should agree upon and follow a clear procedure.

Keeping files this organized is easy once everyone understands the system. The case manager may have to go in and sort things out occasionally, but everyone should attempt consistency in naming and record keeping.

Don't forget to back up digital files. After the subfolders and files are created, they should be immediately backed up to CD, DVD, an external hard drive, or an online file storage service. CDs and DVDs can be stored with the rest of the case's hard files. Make two copies just to be safe.

Part 5
PSYCHIC SKILLS: SENSITIVE TO THE SUPERNATURAL

If you have experienced paranormal phenomena, you may be confused, frightened, and perhaps even a little fearful of being ridiculed. Or you may have just discovered that you are a little bit psychic. The best defense against fear of the unknown is to educate yourself.

It is possible to hone your natural observational skills and objectivity and train yourself to develop whatever latent psychic skills you may already have. In *The Everything® Psychic Book: Tap Into Your Inner Power and Discover Your Inherent Abilities* by Michael R. Hathaway, you'll find a great deal of helpful information.

If you are eager to develop your natural psychic talents, you must ask yourself why. If you wish to explore the boundaries of human consciousness and connect with higher realms—if your intentions are honest and not selfish—you can proceed with confidence. It's hypothesized that everyone has some amount of psychic ability, but the extent of the development of these talents can vary widely.

39. Intuition or Coincidence?

Some people are born with a unique sensitivity to the super-natural and some develop it through hard work and rigorous training. We have all experienced this sixth sense at one point or another. For instance, we know who is calling when the phone rings, or a commercial we are thinking about suddenly appears on the television. These sorts of things happen often in our daily lives, and we chalk them up to coincidence. Some-times that's just what it is.

But if this sixth sense does exist and isn't just coincidence, how can you plug it into your intellect to help you interpret paranormal or psychic data correctly? Here are the first steps to developing your intuition and sensitivity:

1. Acknowledge that the ability exists. Without this vital first step, you cannot move forward and trust the information you're receiving.
2. Listen to your gut feeling. Intuition comes in flashes. When it sweeps over you, note it. Analyze it. Respect it.
3. Engage your intellect. It must be brought in to analyze the information correctly. Trust that something sig-nificant has occurred and attempt to figure out exactly what it means.

Remember that in order for your mind to listen to your intuitive feelings, it must value those feelings. Your mind needs a logical reason to value the information. The best way to convince your mind to pay attention to intuitions is to introduce it to the origins of these feelings.

40. Tapping the Source

Where does psychic or intuitive information come from? Three main theories exist:

1.   The first theory posits that our minds are like organic computers that store the details of every experience we've ever had. Our conscious minds allow us to quietly store all this extra data in our huge biological hard drive. If the subconscious is prompted, it will allow the conscious mind the necessary access to all kinds of helpful information.

2.   A second hypothesis posits that thoughts are energy. They have a bandwidth or frequency similar to a broadcast signal. When others are operating at the same bandwidth, we may experience a bleed-through effect, much like hearing two radio stations at once. This can be called telepathy, or ESP. Some have speculated that this is what creates mass consciousness, also known as groupthink. This is the phenomenon of a large number of people thinking in similar ways. These mental energy signals may subsequently influence many aspects of our lives: social and moral values, politics, and religious beliefs. It is just a theory, but it well might be one explanation for some very disturbing periods in human

history, such as the rise of Nazi Germany, where certain beliefs seemed contagious. If we can consciously tune in or block the signal, we are in much better control of our thoughts and intuitions.

3.   The third source of psychic intuition may come from the superconscious. It is theorized that everyone has access to a higher source of knowledge. Information from the superconscious level of psychic guidance is said to influence your consciousness for your own higher good and helps you make observations and choices from a fresh perspective. This influence can be perceived as an inspiration, warning, or sudden flash of insight.

41. Types of Psychic Abilities

Four basic kinds of psychic ability exist, and people can develop one or more of them. The four psychic senses are psychic feeling, psychic knowing, psychic seeing, and psychic hearing.

+ *Clairsentience, or psychic feeling:* The sense of psychic feeling is what people mean when they say they have a gut feeling or a hunch. When people have a feeling something is about to go wrong, they often experience a sinking feeling in the pit of their stomach.
+ *Claircognizance, or psychic knowing:* Psychic intuition is similar to psychic feeling, but there is no physical sensa-

tion involved; the person simply knows an event is about to take place.

+ *Clairvoyance, or psychic seeing:* This is perhaps the best known psychic skill. When you have a psychic vision, it is as if you're viewing the scene through your mystical eye, or third eye. This is located between your eyebrows and is said to be a powerful psychic tool. Often, you will experience a very brief flash of an object or person. The image slips away if you try too hard to grasp it. People who are clairvoyant often see auras (glowing energy fields) around people, and even plants and animals.

+ *Clairaudience, or psychic hearing:* Psychic hearing occurs when you hear a voice that isn't actually there. People who have clairaudience say it is as if they are hearing a voice inside their head, perhaps just above their ears. A very common clairaudient experience is hearing your name called even though no one is there. This can happen as you're falling asleep, and it is very startling. Another frequent occurrence is parents who believe they hear their children crying or calling to them when they are totally out of earshot.

42. Psychics and Seers

Since the dawn of time, some people have been attuned to events that are inaccessible to the average person. These people have often been consulted and exploited for their talents, but they have also been regarded with suspicion, fear, and sometimes contempt. It is small wonder that many psychics simply chose to keep their knowledge to themselves. At many times, during the medieval era and even as recently as seventeenth-century America, people with these paranormal abilities were burned at the stake or suffered other dreadful fates for the audacity of showing their abilities.

Today we are somewhat more civilized and more tolerant of those who are a little different. Sure, skeptics may scoff, but that has never killed anyone.

Psychics and seers generally fall into three categories:

1. The real deal
2. Total charlatans
3. People with actual abilities who for unknown reasons cheat

How do you tell the real psychics from the frauds? Use your own powers of perception. Just as when you're trying to determine if a client is a hoaxer, ask yourself if you have a gut feeling about the psychic. Does she make you feel uneasy or try to frighten or intimidate you? Does she ask you for money or request that you do something that is against your better judgment? If yes, you should leave the presence of this person as quickly and politely as you can. Even if she truly does have psychic powers, she can have a negative effect on your energy and senses.

You will sense that a genuine psychic or seer is surrounded by a special energy. Although you may be nervous, you should not feel threatened or afraid. A good psychic is usually a good person who has taken all the steps required to build his psychic talents. He meditates to learn to place himself in a receptive state of mind, and he has also learned the skill of creative visualization. He studies, practices, and eventually grows in skill and accuracy over time.

Both the real psychics and frauds sometimes use special tools, such as pendulums, crystal balls, or cards in their work. These tools can help focus concentration and assist in visualization, which is helpful for clairvoyants.

Sadly, there have been psychics with genuine abilities who chose to exploit them. When their powers failed them, they were so invested in their situations that they tried to cover up their loss with chicanery. These people have done a lot of harm to themselves and others and should be avoided.

43. Necromancy: Talking with the Dead

Divination is a way of gathering information by paranormal means, using tools and symbols to acquire knowledge from the collective unconscious, superconscious, or beings on a different plane of existence. This knowledge can be about people, places, and things. It can be gathered from the past, present, and future.

Necromancy is a term used for divination by means of communication with the dead. The tools of divination have their roots in antiquity. Since the dawn of time, humans have tried to contact and control the spirits of the dead.

The most famous tool of the necromancer is the Ouija board. According to some sources, the first historical mention of something resembling a Ouija board was found in China around 1200 B.C.E., a divination method called Fu Ji. But the first use of the Ouija board we're familiar with, named for the French and German words for "yes," occurred during the spiritualist movement of the nineteenth century, when its widespread use was considered harmless. Today it has come into disfavor, as it is said to open a door to poltergeists and other low-level psychic phenomena. This door, once opened, is not easily shut, so the use of the Ouija board is considered dangerous by most psychic investigators and its use seriously discouraged.

The board's surface has the letters of the alphabet, the numerals 0 through 9, and the words "yes," "no," "hello," and "goodbye." A triangular device called a planchette, usually made of plastic and about four inches long, has enough room for two people to lightly rest their fingers on. The planchette has three felt-tipped legs that glide over the board's surface to point at letters, spelling out answers to questions asked by participants.

In his article, "Ouija, Not a Game," writer Dale Kaczmarek of the Ghost Research Society warns that automatic writing and séances are all dangerous for novice users. Kaczmarek suggests that spirits from the lower astral plane are the entities most often attracted by these divination tools, and they introduce chaotic and sometimes even dangerous energy into the homes of the naive. If a psychic or medium is present, she can better control the situation, but extreme caution is still needed.

Don't be tempted to use these devices without the proper safe-guards and training. They have a long history of trouble.

In 1882, physiologist William Carpenter explained such diverse events as the movement of the Ouija board's planch-ette, the circular motion of the pendulum, and even the table tipping of the mediums of his day as the result of something he called "ideomotor action." This term refers to involuntary and unconscious muscle movements on the part of people participating in these activities. Carpenter argued that these unconscious muscular movements could be involuntarily ini-tiated by the mind and then interpreted by participants as paranormal.

As plausible as this explanation may sound, there have been many documented cases of table tipping so extreme that the idea that small muscle movements caused them is simply ludicrous. And if the Ouija board spells out answers to ques-tions that none of the participants knew the answer to and are later verified as true, what are we to think of that?

44. Map Dowsing

Dowsing is another form of divination used since ancient times to seek answers to questions. The first recorded use of dowsing may be found in a cave painting at Tassili Najjer in the Sahara, dated to approximately 6000 B.C.E. It shows a crowd gathered to watch a dowser at work. Ancient people frequently used dowsing rods to locate water.

Probably used initially to determine the will of the gods or find answers to questions about the future, dowsing is used most widely today to locate things. Whether they search for water, oil, or precious metals, dowsers use a forked L-shaped rod or a straight rod to find the material they are looking for.

It has long been debated whether dowsing is an electromagnetic phenomena or an actual paranormal ability. Regardless, the process has sustained the test of time, despite its many detractors.

Sometimes pendulums of metal or crystal are used to dowse, particularly when the dowser is hoping to locate something on a map. Controversial psychic Uri Geller has stated on many occasions that the bulk of his income comes from dowsing to locate oil fields for the petroleum industry.

In the 1970s, Geller underwent double-blind tests in which he was asked to locate either a ball bearing, water, or a magnet concealed within identical metal containers. A third party placed the items in the containers, and scientists filmed Geller as tests were run repeatedly. Geller used a form of dowsing and correctly located the items in almost all of the tests. The scientists determined that the odds were a trillion to one that he had obtained his results by chance.

No one really knows how the dowsing process works. Is the subconscious moving the pendulum, or is a spirit or higher force doing it? Is it biofeedback and bioenergy? Theories and speculation continue.

Perhaps the simplest way for beginners to learn to dowse is with a pendulum. You need a pendulum (metal bobber or crystal) and a chain or string to suspend it from. Make sure you're comfortable with the dowsing tool and are away from any noise, distractions, or electronic equipment.

1.   Determine a system for yourself—for instance, clockwise may mean yes, counterclockwise no.
2.   Relax by taking three or four long, deep breaths.
3.   Begin the experiment by holding the chain or string of the pendulum in your dominant hand about two inches away from the dangling object or bobber.
4.   Break the east-west motion by making a deliberate movement either clockwise or counterclockwise. Hold the pendulum over your other hand.
5.   Ask yourself how the movement feels. Does it feel natural? If not, hold the string or chain a bit higher and keep on going until you find the position that feels right to you and allows the weight on the chain to rotate freely.
6.   Mark that place on the chain or string with permanent marker or a straight pin.
7.   Start your dowsing session by asking simple "yes" or "no" questions.
8.   Make note of the answers and the day's date.

What sort of questions should you ask? Don't get into dark areas, and try to keep the questions simple. If you're looking for employment, you can start by asking, "Will I find work in the next three months?" If the answer is yes, then narrow it down even further: "Will I get work in the next month?" Don't ask complex questions with open-ended responses that can't be answered properly with a simple yes or no, such as, "How much money will the job pay?"

In dowsing, as in so many things in life, practice makes perfect. Inevitably, people who have some luck at dowsing begin to ask for information about the future. Be aware and guard yourself against the influence of negative responses. Real danger exists for those who are sensitive to negative news. Remember that the answers you get about future events are only possibilities of what is to come and are not written in stone. Remember that free will and corrective actions in the present can change what is still to come. In other words, if you don't like the answers you get, use your free will to make choices that will change the outcome.

45. Scrying

Scrying is another form of divination, often used to foretell the future and communicate with the spirit world. Scrying was used by ancient cultures from Persia to Greece to Egypt as a tool for prognostication or predicting future events. Spirits were thought to have a hand in conveying the messages.

Nostradamus, arguably the most famous psychic of all time, was said to have used a small bowl of water as his means of seeing into the future. From the Middle Ages to present times, scrying has been widely used by wizards, witches, clairvoyants, and psychics.

Scryers most often use crystal balls or black mirrors, although any reflective media, even ink, water, and crystals, can be used.

Most people are familiar with the image of the gypsy fortune-teller gazing raptly into a crystal ball to relate the fate of her gullible clientele.

The premise behind scrying is that when the person gazes into the reflective surface in the proper state of relaxation, she will see images that unfold either before her or in her mind's eye—glimpses of a future time, a far-off place, or a past event.

Part 6

SELF-DEFENSE AND PROTECTION

Paranormal activity can range from harmless residual hauntings to potentially harmful poltergeists and malevolent entities. You and your team will want to be prepared for your first encounter with malevolent or inhuman spirits. Thoroughly research the topic and use whatever spiritual protection you deem appropriate.

Each investigator should prepare himself or herself psychologically. Regular investigators may say a simple prayer for protection or perform a ritual, such as carrying a protective medal or amulet. For some, preparing themselves is as simple as mentally invoking the powers of light and keeping a positive mindset.

One of the most basic skills anyone on a case can learn is grace under fire. Sometimes the atmosphere on a case is so highly charged with negativity and fear that it is uncomfortable for even seasoned investigators to stay near it and persevere. The ability to master one's own fears is the mark of an experienced investigator. However, sometimes it is totally appropriate—even necessary—to get out.

46. Basic Protection

What are some of the simplest things you can do to protect yourself before commencing an investigation?

+ Many paranormal investigators say a simple prayer of protection before starting the night's activities. They ask for protection from anything that might harm them during the hunt and from entities that might become attached to them and decide to follow them home.

+ Many ghost hunters would not dream of heading out without holy water, rosaries, and scapulars. These symbols of faith work best for those who believe in them. Every professional paranormal investigative team should have a specialist within their group or on call who can deal with demonic attacks that are extreme enough to require the use of these holy symbols. Ed and Lorraine Warren, the parapsychologists who handled the Amityville Horror case, were staunch Catholics who saw their faith as protection from demonic elements, as do many ghost hunters in the twenty-first century. Even non-Catholics will sometimes carry holy water. If it works, it works.

+ Meditation and/or visualization can be more effective than you suspect. Nelia Petit recommends protecting yourself by invoking the white light of God or the Goddess, either through visualization or spoken words. Kym Black of The Rhode Island Paranormal Research Group (T.R.I.P.R.G.) performs a meditation in which she bathes in white light and dons psychic armor, replete with mirrors to repel malevolent entities, before an investigation.

47. Invoking St. Michael

Exorcists of all persuasions invoke St. Michael the Archangel's name as protection against the dark forces. He is viewed as a potent symbol of good and the leader of the armies of powerful angelic forces—a key player in the battle of good versus evil.

In 1888, Pope Leo XIII collapsed after a morning mass and appeared to be dead. After reviving, he repeated a bizarre conversation he said he had overheard, coming from near the tabernacle. Two voices conversed, voices the Pope alleged were those of Jesus Christ and the Devil. The Devil boasted that he could destroy the Church if he were granted seventy-five years to carry out his plan. He asked permission for "a greater influence over those who will give themselves to my service." In response, Jesus reportedly replied, "You will be given the time and the power."

Pope Leo XIII was so alarmed by what he had heard that he composed the Prayer to St. Michael the Archangel and gave a papal order that it was to be recited after all Low Masses. This was done until 1960, when Pope John XXIII rescinded the order.

Here is a brief version of the prayer that you can use before you begin your investigation, or during it if you sense the need for protection.

PRAYER TO ST. MICHAEL
Saint Michael the Archangel,
defend us in battle.
Be our protection against the wickedness and snares of the devil.
May God rebuke him, we humbly pray;
and do Thou, O Prince of the Heavenly Host—
by the Divine Power of God—
cast into hell, Satan and all the evil spirits,
who roam throughout the world seeking the ruin of souls.
Amen.

48. When the Hunter Becomes the Hunted

Psychics, sensitives, and ghost hunters have existed for hundreds of years in cultures all over the world, so the practices employed to protect them vary according to culture and era. Even some of today's scientific ghost hunters say a prayer of protection before beginning the hunt.

In *Journeys Out of the Body*, Robert Monroe describes his personal experiences of a psychic assault while astral traveling. He describes "rubbery entities" that kept attacking him and attempting to climb onto his back. Eventually, a man in a monk's robe came out and pulled the creatures away, to Monroe's great relief.

Are these nonphysical beings ghosts, demons, spirits, or elementals? What do they gain by attacking or preying on humans and what form do these attacks take? The creatures that prey on living humans are characterized differently, but whether these entities are demons or simply the souls of terribly wicked humans, the net effect is the same. Just as there are good and bad people, there are good and bad spirits that inhabit the other side. Investigating the occult can be likened to opening a door or leaving your doors and windows open to intruders. Unless you take steps to lock the doors and windows you have opened, you may find yourself playing host to unwanted intruders. This has happened over and over again, and is mentioned repeatedly in most literature that deals with the paranormal.

Only very foolish or immature people dabble in the occult without proper preparation and precautions. The classic case is when parents buy a Ouija board for their children to play with, as if it is a game of Monopoly. When problems arise from the opening of a conduit, it sometimes takes a very long time and a lot of effort to shut down that pipeline. Asking for protection and taking proper precautions should be done before any sort of interaction with the spirit realm; this includes reading tarot cards, dowsing, or any sort of divination.

49. Psychic Attack

Anyone can experience psychic attack. Mediums and sensitives are often the targets for this sort of attack because they are such open channels for energy and they often find themselves in circumstances involving disturbing phenomena. If they are wise, they learn to take psychic countermeasures to stop these threats, which can take the form of any number of terrifying visions and feelings. Nelia Petit, a psychic, medium, and paranormal investigator, has been the target of psychic attacks many times in the course of her work and has helped people escape supernatural oppression. Petit has a spirit guide who shields her from the worst aspects of the attacks, but she is still vulnerable. She has seen horrible visions of her dogs and even her mother lying slaughtered in her home. Petit usually ignores such things, but also finds that anger is a helpful response. It seems to drive the entity and its negative influence away. Once she even heard an entity whisper, "I think I'll go for a little ride, I'll be back." She resisted the urge to pick up the phone and call her husband, John. She didn't want the entity to know that it had successfully pushed her buttons with its implied threat.

Petit has been plagued by a shadowy figure who lingers outside her door. She claims that after weeks of harassment, she decided to go into a trance to confront the entity. Petit grappled with the figure and dragged him toward the light, where someone helped her by pulling the entity through and into the light. Because the transition has to be voluntary, this being was able to escape and has returned to continue harassing her.

In her experience, Petit believes that psychics are vulnerable to attack and can even be hurt physically when they attract the attention of entities on the other side, both good and bad. All psychics agree that allowing yourself to be intimidated is the worst possible response, as fear opens a point of vulnerability that can be further exploited. Once the primal emotion of fear is triggered, the entity has a handle it can use to do further damage.

It is possible, according to sensitives, to be on the lookout for psychic attack. They say warning signs may come in the form of a prolonged spell of depression, anxiety, or anger. If the person experiencing the attack suddenly realizes how uncharacteristic her behavior is, she can take steps to undo the damage.

As in other areas of paranormal investigation, rule out the natural explanations before jumping to the conclusion that you are under attack. A tummy ache or a creepy feeling isn't necessarily paranormal. Warning signs of a psychic attack include:

- *Tiredness and fatigue.* In this frequent form of psychic attack, energy is drained from the victim. He may even have a strange sense of detachment, as if the things that are happening around him are unreal. Feeling drained and exhausted without good reason is an indication that something strange may be going on, and a psychic attack may be occurring.
- *Physical ailments.* Headache, stomach ailments, and unexplained pains may be symptoms of psychic attack. If a person, place, or thing consistently causes a negative physical reaction, consider the possibility that a supernatural situation may be the reason.
- *Persistent or recurring bad dreams.* If you have never been prone to nightmares and suddenly you dream of being hunted or oppressed, you might be experiencing psychic attacks in your dreams.
- *Physical sensations.* Strange physical sensations in the solar plexus may be a sign that someone or something

is interfering with your energy field. The warning sign starts as a tightening in the abdomen. Shaking or trembling, coldness in the extremities, and a sudden, unbearably anxious feeling of panic may also be signs of psychic attack.

50. Dealing with Psychic Oppression

Experienced investigators in the field of the paranormal know what to look for and how to counteract the early signs of psychic trouble in an investigation. Depression, despair, and persistent anxiety are all signs. An effective way of dealing with psychic oppression and attack is to ask yourself what could have triggered the feeling you are having or the streak of very bad luck you are experiencing. If there is no logical, natural explanation, what remains must be paranormal in nature.

Most groups have people they can call on for assistance when this situation occurs. It might be a group member or a cleric or demonologist the group uses for consultation. Whoever it is, she will be called in to sort out the situation and send the oppressive presence packing. Usually, things are put back in order very quickly.

Prolonged depression and anxiety that arises in those who have been around paranormal activity may be a sign that more is going on than is first understood. A state of depression, sometimes bordering on the suicidal, may be triggered by an encounter with demonic or elemental energies. Always advise clients to seek medical or psychological help if they are in danger.

51. Potential Damage from Malevolent Entities

In demonic situations, horrific damage may have been inflicted by the entities. In these cases of possession, the psychological trauma can be extremely devastating to the victims, their families, and the exorcists involved. Fortunately, the victim often experiences amnesia regarding the most horrific aspects of the incident. The rest of the trauma associated with the case may then gradually fade away over time.

Ghouls are entities that do damage of a different sort. They induce feelings of icy coldness, disorientation, and despair. These attacks eat away at the confidence of their victims until they are so demoralized and frightened that they plunge in to a state of deep depression. Although ghosts may be seen, ghouls never manifest, except as a horrible feeling of evil and despair. This entity's influence has been known to drive people to thoughts of suicide. Oddly, the ghoul seems best able to cast its ghastly influence during warm and muggy weather and seems anchored to specific locations, lingering like a bad smell. The area of its influence can be so clearly defined that one can step in and out of its range within a few steps.

52. Physical Attack

As if psychic attack isn't bad enough, investigators can also find themselves being physically attacked. The Rhode Island Paranormal Research Group (T.R.I.P.R.G.) investigators Nelia Petit, Kym Black, and Andrew Laird all recount tales of coming to physical harm when on an investigation. In the most common type of attack, the person is shoved or thrown against a wall. While investigating paranormal activity at the Paine House, Black fell victim to an angry spirit who called her a witch and threw her against a wall, knocking her out. Petit has been thrown to the floor, hurled against a wall, and pushed down a flight of steps.

Laird told of being on an investigation at the Rhode Island Training School when he apparently angered an entity. The 275-pound, 6-foot-5-inch man was picked up and tossed against a wall as if he were a child before being repeatedly hit and punched. He wanted to go to an emergency room but couldn't figure out an explanation for his injuries. As he said, "What are we supposed to tell the doctor? 'We just got our butts kicked by Casper?'"

Amazingly, in none of these cases were any bones broken or any permanent damage done. Petit believes the dark spirits have limits placed on how far they can go when attacking, and the extent of the damage is limited to bumps and bruises.

Sometimes the attacks are not as violent and manifest as dizziness, disorientation, the feeling of bugs crawling over the skin, or a tingling sensation. These weird sensations may also mean a spirit is trying to make contact in the only way it can.

If they are doing physical or psychic damage, it makes very little difference if these attacking entities are ghosts, demons, poltergeists, or elementals. Poltergeists may be the most popularly recognized source of this kind of attack, although poltergeists rarely cause accidents that result in serious injury. Though observers may be struck by flying objects and subjected to glancing blows, people are almost never seriously injured. The rare cases where more serious injuries occur get all the publicity.

These same rules that restrict dark spirits seem to hold true for hauntings, where occasionally the investigators may get punched, clawed, or shoved by an angry entity. In cases of possession requiring an exorcist, claw marks and grotesque swelling may appear, virtually disfiguring the unfortunate victim. If the exorcism is successfully completed, these injuries heal quickly and are soon hardly noticeable. Interestingly, even the fires associated with poltergeist activity are usually quickly discovered and put out.

Tales concerning physical attack usually seem to deal with ghost hunters, as in the instance when a TAPS cameraman was knocked to the ground, or another case when Jason Hawes was bitten on the back. People who have dabbled in the supernatural are also vulnerable to attack. Casual bystanders or observers don't usually seem to elicit the same active hostility that investigators experience.

Accounts of people being physically injured by entities aren't common, but they do exist. The entity usually manifests a furious energy that blasts people off their feet, causing them to bounce off walls. Most ghosts, like most people, are not violent or angry.

But some are. In most cultures around the world, ghosts are thought to have some ill intent toward the living, which they manifest either through inducing a chilling reaction or by doing some sort of physical harm.

Injuries can also occur when reacting to an entity; a trip and fall or taking a tumble down a flight of stairs may be accidental, but the trigger was the paranormal event. Entities have been known to trip or push people. When these attacks occur, serious injury is sometimes only narrowly avoided.

The exception to the no-serious-injury rule is when these entities get a little help from their friends, the demons. Researchers pretty much agree that demonic entities can cause serious harm to humans. Demonic encounters are very, very rare. Most entities encountered are human spirits who have passed over. The overwhelming majority of those spirits are benign and even benevolent. Still, if an individual is exploring high-risk areas or is involved in the practice of dark magic or experimenting with decadent and selfish lifestyles, she may attract the demonic. The best way to stop the attack of elementals and demons is not to draw their attention. If you must, conduct a ritual or procedure to protect yourself before each exposure to the risky situation. This can take many forms, including meditation, purifying with sage smoke, amulets, prayers, or whatever is congruent with your own belief system.

In rare cases, a ghost has become overly territorial and decided that it doesn't want anyone living in its place. Entities of this sort do everything in their power to drive the residents away, including throwing objects at them. Usually, these human entities can be coaxed and cajoled into the light or made to stop their activities through other means, such as rituals to invite them to be at rest and that protect the residents of the house. If a protection ritual fails, then it is time to call in the big guns and ask for outside help. Sensitives often get assistance from their fellow psychics on the investigative team. Kym Black underwent psychic attack and enlisted the aid of fellow The Rhode Island Paranormal Research Group (T.R.I.P.R.G.) members to drive the entity away by using a ritual specially designed to break the tie between the entity and Kym, who bounced back from the oppressive presence within days.

53. Client or Problematic People Issues

Although the field of paranormal investigation is made up largely of people volunteering their time and services, clients are not always grateful and appreciative of their efforts. In some cases, they can be more troublesome than the paranormal.

In one instance, a sound engineer participated in a séance at Belcourt Castle in Newport, Rhode Island. The mansion is said to be haunted by a monk who lingers near the chapel, and a suit of armor from which weird screams occasionally erupt. Two antique chairs are rumored to be strong enough to throw off anyone who dares sit in them.

The sound engineer reported that the energies in the gothic ballroom during the séance were incredibly violent and his sound equipment picked up the howling and moaning sounds. He found himself wishing that the trapped spirits would just go into the light, and he urged them to do so. Afterward, he learned that the sensitive who regularly conducted ghost tours there had complained that he had affected her bread and butter—all the ghosts were gone. He retorted that she didn't have the right to run a paranormal petting zoo. He has since sworn off any sort of paranormal investigation; for weeks after the Belcourt Castle incident, he suffered from a lingering malaise.

54. Guarding Against Equipment Failure

One universal phenomenon ghost hunters have observed: In the presence of the paranormal, technology can behave weirdly. Batteries drain and go dead. Audio recorders fail. Equipment malfunctions. In a practical sense, this means you need backup batteries and backup equipment to record the phenomena that causes the equipment to fail. It also means that you should always bring along some sort of nontechnological means of seeing in the dark, even if it is something as low-tech as matches and candles.

Electronics sometimes seem to attract orb or poltergeist activity, and there have been countless reports of appliances, televisions, and computers being turned on by unseen hands, sometimes even when they are unplugged. But occasionally there is a simple explanation for this. For example, walkie-talkies have been known to act like remote controls and turn on televisions.

In one episode of *Ghost Hunters,* Grant Wilson from TAPS explained his theory about why paranormal activity causes equipment failure. When the paranormal activity at a site is really hot, the entities who are trying to manifest will draw energy from the air around them, causing sudden temperature drops or drained batteries. Sometimes the people in the vicinity will be also be overcome with great fatigue and tiredness, as if something is draining them.

Another theory goes that increased electromagnetic field activity and positive ionization (static electricity) are present at most active paranormal sites. Most of today's digital devices use nickel-cadmium rechargeable batteries, and the battery manufacturers warn that that they are extremely susceptible to both electromagnetic fields and static electricity.

Occasionally, there have been odd reports of batteries operating for far longer than they should or even cases of electrical meters running backward. These may be instances of entities trying to give energy back rather than take it.

It's not just battery drain that stops investigators' work. Occasionally, cameras will work, but a strange blurry effect makes all the images look surreal. This is puzzling to experience, especially to seasoned photographers who know what to expect from their camera under all sorts of lighting conditions.

55. Jinxes and Hexes

We usually think of jinxes as curses placed on one individual by another, but nature spirits and elementals can bring curses or jinxes down on people, too. In Laurens van der Post's book, *The Lost World of the Kalahari*, the author tells the tale of a jinx being placed on his expedition after they broke a native taboo as they traveled across the countryside toward the Slippery Hills in Africa. They were repeatedly attacked by bees and plagued by inexplicable equipment failures. In general, they had nothing but bad luck from the moment they broke the taboo. When they finally accepted that they had violated a strict taboo, they propitiated the spirits of the Slippery Hills and the expedition proceeded without further incident.

In the literature of the supernatural, there are more stories about cursed objects than about cursed people. It only becomes apparent that an object is cursed after it has passed through the hands of several owners, consistently bringing misfortune and injury to them.

In Hawaii, the goddess of the volcano curses those who remove lava rocks. In Europe, there are cursed castles and moors, and in Ireland there are places called raths and fairy rings where the locals will not build for fear of their lives.

Details of how or why objects carry negative energy vary according to location and time period. One single theme seems to apply in most instances, though. A traumatic event imprints itself so thoroughly on the object or surroundings that its negativity becomes permanently associated with it. Take the case of James Dean's cursed Porsche, for example.

After James Dean died in a car crash in 1955, the Porsche was sold to a garage owner. It slipped as it was being unloaded and a mechanic standing nearby suffered two broken legs. The car was chopped up for parts and the engine from the Porsche was sold to a doctor who was into racing. Subsequently, the car he had put the engine into went out of control, killing him and seriously injuring the driver of another car in the race, which just happened to have the drive shaft from Dean's car in it.

The Porsche's battered body was sold to be used in a movable display for Highway Safety, and it fell off its mounting brackets and broke a teenager's hip in Sacramento. Weeks later, a transport truck carrying Dean's car was in an accident. The truck driver was killed when he was crushed by the car, which came loose and rolled over him. A racecar driver who bought the car's heavy-duty tires was nearly killed when all the tires blew out simultaneously for no apparent reason.

In Oregon, a truck carrying the car slipped its handbrake and crashed into a store. On display in New Orleans, it mysteriously broke into eleven pieces. Perhaps everyone breathed a sigh of relief when the car mysteriously disappeared while being transported by train back to Los Angeles.

56. Possession

Largely unknown to the public before the premiere of the 1973 film *The Exorcist*, possession cases have been around for millennia. Although there are many recorded instances of benevolent possession, most of the cases that require treatment by an exorcist are of an extremely harmful and alarming nature. Cases of possession may be on the rise globally in the new millennia. Some psychologists attribute claims of possession to the stress of modern life and drug use; others point to increased diagnoses of dissociative disorders, which cause sudden disruptions in psychological function.

It seems inevitable that many so-called cases of demonic possession are in actuality merely graphic examples of auto-suggestion or hysteria. This is where today's ghost hunters must exhibit their expertise. If someone is behaving very oddly, it must first be determined if it is a case of possession or mental illness. Only after all the logical explanations are dismissed can the occasional valid case of possession be identified.

Possession isn't always by evil spirits or demons, either. In many cultural traditions, possession is not thought to be demonic. Reports of spontaneous and deliberate possession are found throughout history and throughout the world. In more primitive societies, it is considered a form of shamanism and is likely the world's oldest spiritual tradition.

57. Calling in Priests and Clergy

When psychic and physical attacks have gotten out of control, most investigative groups will call in help from specialists—the demonologists, clergy, or shamans who deal with these things on a routine basis. The very idea that evil—in whatever form your religion or culture perceives it—can inhabit humans against our will is a terribly frightening concept. It is an idea so alarming that we usually seek protection from it through the representatives of organized religions, one of the most common of which is, of course, the Roman Catholic Church.

Paranormal investigator and founder of The Rhode Island Paranormal Research Group Andrew Laird has a friend who is a Catholic priest. He is available to help T.R.I.P.R.G. if the group encounters anything that even smacks of the demonic. Laird says, "Any priest or ordained Christian minister can be an exorcist, so I am told. I have seen both at work and really there is little difference. With that said, I have been with Father John while he has taken part in exorcisms, but he does not consider himself an exorcist per se but an assistant."

The Catholic Church has recently stepped up its response to potential demonic possession. The *Daily Mail*, a British newspaper, reported in 2007 that Pope Benedict XVI ordered his bishops to set up exorcism squads to address the rise of Satanism and the increased interest in all things Satanic. The Congregation for the Doctrine of the Faith, a department devoted to overseeing the promotion and safeguarding of the integrity of the faith, has been in existence in some form since 1542. Benedict XVI served as its head from 1982 until 2005, when he became pope.

The late Dr. Malachi Martin was a theologian who spent thirty years as an exorcist. In 1958, Father Martin was in Cairo to study a newly discovered collection of Hebrew writings from the time of Abraham. The trip had a profound impact on him. While he was there, he asked to assist in an exorcism. A young Egyptian man had become so involved in Satanism that he was suspected of being complicit in sacrificing his own sisters.

What Father Martin saw in Egypt convinced him that he had to fight the powers of evil, no matter the personal cost to himself. Some have speculated that Father Martin may have been the inspiration for the older priest in *The Exorcist*.

Before his passing, Father Martin said, "Every exorcism takes something out of you that cannot be put back. The demon goes, but it carries a part of you away with it. A little of the exorcist dies each time. It's a permanent mental fight against a powerful, dangerous enemy."

Do non-Catholic paranormal investigators ever call in Catholic priests? They do indeed, but they are just as likely to call in an Episcopal priest or a Jewish rabbi. Even though the Catholic Church has a long history of blessing troubled houses and performing exorcisms, many other churches and clergy members offer these services as well.

58. Wards, Shields, and Visualization

Simply put, wards and shields are selective energy barriers. They can be made of physical substances or they can be forms of thought, like visualizations or prayers. Whatever their form, they all serve as a wall behind which the investigator can take shelter to ward off physical or psychic attack.

Conducting rituals to protect yourself or your home from harm is an ancient practice. Today's investigators draw from many traditions to design rituals that feel right to them and provide the psychic and spiritual strength they need in times of crisis.

Warding and shielding a home can provide protection from negative energies. Many sensitives and paranormal investigators firmly believe they must protect their own energy fields and homes from the intrusion of negative forces before going out on an investigation. Even Christians often invoke the protection of a divine light, which they visualize as a barrier between them and whatever they may encounter in the course of an investigation. The entities and energies they encounter on investigations may not be inherently evil, but frightened and confused spirits can still cause problems. Like confused people, they can lash out and cause harm to innocent bystanders. After a house has been cleared of whatever entities haunted it, a blessing of the house, which acts as a natural ward, should always take place.

Some investigators and sensitives feel it is necessary and prudent to protect their own homes as well as their persons. They develop their own unique systems for this, usually involving the establishment of protective shields and wards. These are highly individualistic and should be crafted to fill the needs of the practitioner.

Here are some basic facts about wards:

+ Warding allows positive energy to be retained; it keeps good energy from escaping but also allows it in.
+ Warding blocks negative energy and keeps harmful and disruptive energy at bay.
+ Selective wards may block certain energies while permitting others to pass; some energy is even transmuted according to the needs of the occupants.

This sort of warding requires quite a bit of research and a high degree of sophistication to carry out. Some people are able to fine-tune the porosity of their wards to let only the energy they want into their home environment, almost like a strainer. They keep out unwanted energy, and of course, different people will want to keep out different types of energy.

Visualizing shields around the outside or home can prove very effective. An image of armor plates is a very effective protective visualization; people employ it for protection of their bodies as well as their houses. Mirrors, force fields, and thick stone walls are also effective images. These shields should be recharged periodically to maintain their effectiveness. A bubble of white light around the entire body, rather like the one surrounding Glinda in *The Wizard of Oz*, is one of the most common visualizations.

59. Using Sigils and Charms

In the field of paranormal investigating, it is not unusual to find people carrying lucky charms and other protective items such as *sigils* (a symbol or sign often believed to possess magical powers). They feel these charms and sigils form an energy barrier and protective shield. Sigils can be etched or engraved on a small object and placed in a central location or etched on some part of the house to be protected. Sigils are encoded with intentions and used primarily for defense and protection. They are drawn on the outer walls of the house or inscribed on four pieces of metal and then placed at the four corners of the site.

Simple charms placed around the house, especially at key points like doors, windows, and corners, can be very effective. Little mirrors placed above doors and windows to deflect incoming negative energy work well, too. Wind chimes and other angelic, dangling, or sparkly items can be hung around the home to keep the energy fresh and positive. This is something akin to the principle of breaking up stagnant chi in Feng Shui. Additionally, plants can act like canaries in a coal mine. They absorb negative energy, so placing them around your home can be an effective way of detecting an influx of negative energy. If they seem ill for no apparent reason, you may take it as a warning that something negative is affecting the house.

Charms and amulets many thousands of years old have been found in tombs in ancient Egypt. They were routinely interred with the dead, hidden in mummy wrappings. It is believed that the living used them both as protection against evil and as a way of attracting good fortune.

Amulets and talismans have been used for millennia to protect the wearer from evil spirits, sorcery, and other harmful paranormal phenomena. Depending on the culture, these wards can take many forms. Horns, evil eyes, and scarabs are still in use today.

60. Cleansing Techniques and Rituals

Recently, a cultural consensus seems to have emerged, at least among those in the paranormal community, concerning what is deemed proper procedure after an investigation. Most groups indicate that they think it is wise to bless the house, its inhabitants, and themselves at the end of an investigation. These rituals can range from the simplest to the most complex and differ widely from group to group and region to region.

Blessing, also called cleansing, is a removal of anything unwanted that you've brought away from the site with you. The most important thing about a cleansing ritual is that the intention of the people doing it is clear and strong. Minor elements, such as an essential oil, can be missing as long as the intention is uppermost in the participants' minds and the goal of the cleansing is positive.

THREE TYPES OF PERSONAL CLEANSING

- ✦ *Bathing.* A bath with Epsom salts or cleansing herbs serves to remove the last traces of any physical contamination. The soothing scents of the herbs are grounding and make it easy for the investigator to achieve a focused state of mind.
- ✦ *Saging.* A sort of bath without water, saging can be done either individually or in a group and has much the same function as a bath in water. The smoke from burning sage provides a physical barrier and the scent provides a mental clarity and relaxation that allow the investigator to erect a barrier of protection. The dried leaves are rolled into a long bundle called a wand. When they are lit, they emit an incense-like smoke. The smoke of the sage plant can be used to cleanse both people and spaces. In cultures around the world, sage has been used as a cleansing herb for centuries.
- ✦ *Prayer or spell.* Often preceded by bathing or saging, a prayer or spell provides a clear channel of good intention and integrates the positive energies into a force for good.

House Cleansing Ritual

If you feel that something unpleasant or unwanted has followed you home, you may want to cleanse your home.

BLESSING SUPPLIES

+ An incense burner or censer (a brass incense burner on a metal chain, which can be carried around the house safely—any other type of incense burner should be placed on a small tray)
+ Sea salt
+ A white candle in a candleholder
+ A broom made from natural, not synthetic, materials (such as willow or hazel)
+ Matches or lighters and a candlesnuffer
+ Incense (frankincense, myrrh, sandalwood, lavender, or sage, either in stick or powdered form)
+ Charcoal block (for powdered incense)
+ A large crystal
+ A plain ceramic bowl large enough to hold the crystal and the incense burner
+ Anointing oil, optional (frankincense, myrrh, sandalwood, or lavender)

1. Assemble your materials on a table or other flat surface. If several people are participating, gather them together near the table. Nonparticipants should leave the premises until the ritual is completed.

2.   Place a few drops of oil on the candle. Light the candle and the incense.

3.   Put the salt in the bottom of the bowl. Place the crystal an inch deep in the salt. If you do not have a censer, place the incense burner in the bowl as well. Place these items in the center of the table with the broom in front of them.

4.   Concentrate on the broom, bowl, and candle, picturing them all surrounded by a cleansing, bright-white light. Let this light expand outward to encompass the whole house. As it does so, it will permeate every corner, nook, and cranny.

5.   Pick up the broom and sweep counterclockwise around the entire house, starting at the front door. Continue until you have completed a circle that brings you back to the front door. As you sweep, imagine all impurities being propelled out of the house, and repeat, "By the power of all things holy and good, by the sea and the stars, by earth, air, fire, and water, be gone, all unclean things!"

6.   Sweep the bad things out of the door and out of the house. Return to the candle and incense. Pick up the incense and walk clockwise around the interior of the house three times, allowing the smoke to pervade each corner. As you walk, offer a blessing: "May this house be filled with light, love, and laughter, so full that all else is driven out. By the power of all things holy and good, by the sea and the stars, by earth, air, fire, and water, be gone, all unclean things!"

7. An additional prayer may be offered, linked to the religious tradition of the practitioner, such as, "In the name of Jesus Christ, amen." Or, "Blessed be!"

8. Conceal the crystal in the center of the home as a sort of ward against negative energy. Place a pinch of salt in four tiny bowls at each corner of the house. Snuff out the candle.

Part 7

INVESTIGATIVE WORK: RESEARCH AND LEGALITIES

All investigators should develop the proper protocols and approach the paranormal with an attitude of respect and responsibility. As people add to their knowledge of the super-natural realm, they should be careful in their procedures. Knowledge is power when dealing with the unknown; the more investigators know the better researchers and ghost hunters they become. Aspiring investigators put themselves and others at risk when they don't bring a sense of seriousness and responsibility to their research.

61. Handling a Request to Investigate

When a request to investigate comes in, the case manager will take down the information about what is happening. During a request-to-investigate interview, the case manager should ask the potential client the following questions:

1. What sort of phenomena are you experiencing? Are there moving shadows or are you glimpsing something out of the corner of your eye?
2. Do you ever experience unexplained cold spots?
3. Do you hear footsteps or other unexplained noises, such as tapping or voices saying your name?
4. Do your children ever report seeing someone who isn't there?
5. Do animals seem to follow something you can't see with their eyes or have a fearful reaction without any apparent reason?
6. Have you noticed any strange odors?
7. Do things disappear and then inexplicably reappear later?
8. Do you ever feel you are being watched?

If the client answers yes to more than three of the questions, the case manager should schedule an investigation for the near future. If there are children in the home or a sense of peril, the investigation should be scheduled immediately.

Some groups ask for as much background information as they can get, such as the age of the site, what sort of sounds have been heard, and what abnormalities have been seen. If there is sufficient time, a researcher should look into the history of the house or site at reference libraries and historical societies. Every little tidbit of information may be of importance in figuring out exactly what is happening at the allegedly haunted location.

People who contact ghost hunters and paranormal investigators are sometimes quite desperate. They have reached the end of their ropes emotionally; in some cases, they really fear they are losing their minds. They may have had no experience with the supernatural before, so they have no context for what is happening. They are often referred by clergy and will be desperate to tell their stories to the investigators in hope of finding some relief from the chaos and fear that accompanies paranormal situations.

Not all the detective work is yours to do! A client statement can be one of the most valuable documents in your reference file. Before the team arrives at the site, the potential client should be asked to organize the information about what he has witnessed and to prepare at least a rough chronology of events. Some groups ask for a report to be written before they come out to do the investigation; others will bring a form with them and interview the person or persons involved in the incidents.

62. Assessing the Threat Level

Perhaps the most important question of all concerns how the client feels about what she is experiencing. Does she feel threatened? Based on the client's answers to these questions, the case manager will decide whether the respondent is sincere and credible. If she seems to be, then an investigation is planned.

When interviewing, different protocols are required for different cases, depending on the urgency of the situation. Many paranormal groups will drop everything to come to the assistance of families with children, or if there seems to be a risk of imminent harm to the occupants of an allegedly haunted home. Make sure you or your group have a clear sense of what kinds of cases require different responses.

The threat level can be assessed after the client interview. Sometimes, investigators may suspect that there isn't a threat at all. In most cases, the activity being investigated does not turn out to be paranormal, but can be debunked as a normal occurrence that has been mistakenly perceived as supernatural.

The team will assess what is happening and will confer about the information gained from the interview and during the preliminary research. They then design a plan for conducting the investigation and attempt to make an initial classification of the entities that might be involved.

63. The On-Site Interview

After gathering preliminary information and assessing the threat level, the interviewers proceed to the site and meet with the client there. Occasionally, another in-depth interview takes place on-site, and team members are thoroughly briefed on the case. Pertinent follow-up questions are asked simply to verify the witness' first account of the phenomena. Before you invest much time and energy in a case, you should be sure that something real is occurring and that the ghost-hunting team is not being set up or tricked.

The interviewer should speak with every member of the household. Everyone who is in any way a participant—either a victim of or a witness to the activity—should be interviewed. If young children are involved, they may be very disturbed to speak about their experiences or reluctant to respond to the interviewer's queries, so investigators must exercise a great deal of discretion and skill while gently interviewing children.

A great deal of information can come out during these interviews, and clients are relieved to be able to talk freely about their experiences to people who will believe them. They may really open up.

Take notes on the interviews and record all the pertinent facts for reference later. Occasionally, some clients may at first deny, then reluctantly admit, that they have been involved in some sort of experimentation, such as using a Ouija board or holding a séance, that opened the door for entities to walk through. Sometimes the clients are reluctant to make the admission in front of other family members or housemates. This is where follow-up conversations by team members are quite helpful.

If more than one person has seen or experienced something paranormal, each person should be interviewed separately. Investigators should compare the interviews to catch discrepancies or find points of congruency. These reports should be as detailed and comprehensive as possible; they will help you understand the chronology of the phenomena. They should contain the approximate date of the onset of the activity, with a full description of the paranormal events.

Investigators should ask for further details about sounds heard and things seen, smelled, or even sensed. People will sometimes mention a feeling of being watched or a feeling of extreme fear. Often, they will mention cold spots or extreme temperature shifts. Investigators should question individuals about any event that might have triggered the activity. The following questions can be used as a starting point:

+ Was a séance held or Ouija board used before the disturbance began?
+ Did someone die in the house recently? Did someone die in the house any time in its history?
+ Has anyone been physically harmed: scratched, bitten, or slapped?
+ Has anyone had disturbing or frightening dreams?
+ Are there reports of unexplained fires or objects that have disappeared?
+ Do any pets live in the household? If so, are there any areas they avoid or growl at consistently?

As the investigation begins, clients generally either go off-site or get out of the team's way. Each team member makes his own preparations, part of which is doing preliminary readings and keeping notes of his individual experiences during the investigation. In their diaries or work logs, the individuals involved in the investigation will record which pieces of equipment they used and make careful notes of any unexplained phenomena they may have personally experienced.

64. Understanding the Site Layout and Location

When interviewing clients on-site, have them show you around the location, pointing out areas that may be of particular interest. In small homes and businesses, the setup and floor plans may be so simple there is no concern about team members tripping over obstacles or getting lost in a maze of interconnected rooms. But in large older buildings, even seasoned investigators easily lose their bearings.

Site layout becomes a real issue when it comes to setting up electronic surveillance equipment, with cords and power lines snaking through doorways and corridors. The best locations for the equipment must be planned quite carefully, both to keep the team safe and to optimize the possibility of catching the most paranormal activity.

Determining the locations of power lines and wiring within a building can save investigators many problems and false readings later. Remember, the team is there to debunk the haunting, so eliminating the natural explanations for unusual readings is the first step. Once known sources of EMF spikes and other environmental anomalies have been eliminated, what remains is probably paranormal. You should try to rule out all geomagnetic and geothermal explanations for events. Although instruments that measure electromagnetic fields and temperature fluctuations are considered reliable means of detection, they should be used with caution. Too often, alarmingly high positive readings are only the result of interference from electrical wiring, conduits, or appliances in use in the building. When using any sort of EMF meter, interference from power sources must always be ruled out before drawing any conclusions that they may be of paranormal origin. Any large concentration of metal, such as old iron pipes, fuse boxes, or radiators, can cause magnetic fields that will affect the equipment. Even cell phones can cause small magnetic fields that will affect sensitive equipment.

What generates EMF? Most household appliances, actually. Electricity is the most common source of power and it is easily generated and transmitted. As electricity moves through wires and appliances, an EMF field is generated.

Fortunately, some investigative sites are in old, abandoned locations that have no power sources and are consequently free from any artificial, man-made electrical interference. This simplifies the analysis of unusual EMF readings because it is easier to rule out electrical sources.

It is equally important to track site conditions. During investigations, environmental conditions should always be recorded in an attempt to identify trends or fluctuations that may possibly correspond with paranormal activity. Whenever possible, avoid sites that are open to the elements, as there are so many uncontrollable conditions.

Good investigators try to take baseline readings at the beginning, middle, and end of an investigation, no matter what else is going on. Further readings are taken as investigators explore the site and encounter out-of-the-ordinary situations or activities.

Another factor that must be considered is the geography and geology of the area. Some people suspect that haunting activity takes place more readily near running water. If the building under investigation is near a running stream or brook, or if water runs under the structure, it may help explain what is going on. In the famous case of the Pontefract Poltergeist in Britain, the activity all took place near a small stream. In fact, the property had originally been located practically on top of the site of an old bridge crossing the stream.

Thomas Lethbridge, an archaeologist and historian, spent most of his working life as the keeper of Anglo-Saxon antiquities at Cambridge University Museum. He was one of the first people to theorize that moving water generates a faint magnetic field, which might supply sufficient energy for paranormal entities to manifest. He also thought that lava and quartz rocks could generate mild fields from which entities could draw energy. Lethbridge was one of the first researchers to postulate the existence of ley lines, the hypothetical alignment between underground watercourses and various ancient holy sites. Some people believe ley lines possess a mystical energy, which would explain why so many paranormal events occur in their vicinity.

65. Inform Yourself about the Site Beforehand

Once the decision has been made to proceed with the investigation, gather as much information as possible about the case. Know what you are getting yourself into; find out all you can about the history of the building. Your client is your first source for information about the property, but sometimes she doesn't know the complete story. Particularly in the case of older buildings, the full history may take some digging to uncover.

What shape is the property in, and are there any areas that should be avoided due to safety issues? This could be anything from quicksand on the property to weak floorboards, walls, or ceilings in the building. Safety issues should be discussed with the property owner at the initial interview, and the team members should be briefed immediately prior to starting the investigation. Always be aware of your surroundings. Most investigations are done at night, but a walk-through done under good lighting conditions offers you the opportunity to find and note safety hazards that might go unnoticed in the dark.

Remember that you must have permission to explore a site. If it is necessary to cross someone else's property to gain access to the property you're investigating, or if you are investigating an alleged haunting in an abandoned property or cemetery, be sure to get the proper permissions before setting foot on the site in question. You don't want to get in trouble with property owners or the law.

The popularity of ghost hunting has led to property damage and personal injury in some areas. In an allegedly haunted house in Worthington, Ohio, a homeowner fired shots to scare off a group of self-proclaimed teenage ghost hunters and shot a girl in the head. Trespassing ghost hunters have been arrested in many states. You most certainly don't want to be arrested for trespassing. There are legal repercussions, and it will tarnish your professional reputation. Permission is usually not hard to obtain, and team members work better when they know they have every right to be there.

66. Resources for Background Searches

The researchers should visit the local library and historical society, if there is one in the area, to check on the background of the property. Because hauntings often occur in older properties, it may be necessary to dig quite far back into the property records. If a murder, suicide, or any other traumatic incident occurred on the premises, a search may turn up information that verifies potential paranormal activity. It can also verify names of people or facts involved in the case.

Allot enough time to do this part of the investigation properly; it may take several days of long research to follow the paper trail. You may have to cut through red tape at historical societies, so contact them ahead of time, particularly if they are only open a few days a week or have membership requirements to search their records. State historical societies are a good place to access information if you have the last name of the person for whom you are searching. This can yield the birth and death years and possibly the names of other family members buried nearby.

Place a call to public libraries and ask pertinent questions about their hours and procedures for researchers. They will often have records on microfiche, and most have the local newspaper on file going back to the early days of the community. You can check records to see if anything newsworthy happened in the vicinity of your site.

You can search census records, court records, and birth, marriage, and death records at most county courthouses for a nominal fee. Once you've found out who lived in the house during a given time frame, these records can yield a lot of background information.

This sort of record checking can be very time consuming, especially in big cities where the higher population will mean sifting through a lot more data.

Checking online to see if some of the records might be available through the city or county's Internet site is one way of saving time during this phase of the investigation. Cemetery records are sometimes listed in a database online.

Land records can be a rich source of information about the history and owners of the property in question. These records are kept by the county or city in which the property is located and also include the tax records.

In order to access the records, you may need to provide the legal description of the property; be sure to get that before heading out. Another source of land information is the tax assessment data, which can often be accessed online if you have the property address. These records are kept differently in each locale, but mining them for data can be easy, as there is usually a record of each time a property changed hands, whether through inheritance or sale. Sometimes they contain such important data as the names of co-owners or even floor plans or photos of the house.

Information about the location, such as outbuildings and the condition of the property, can sometimes be ascertained online. Most online databases contain the current property owner's name, the year the property was built, the lot size, the construction material, the number of bedrooms and bathrooms, the square footage, and the type of heating system.

Armed with the knowledge of when the structure was built, you can research the history of residents and any potential past paranormal activity. Occasionally, your research will turn up something significant in the history of the place.

67. Other Sources of Site Information and History

After searching for records on the Internet, looking through microfiche in the library and historical societies, and investigating records at City Hall, what else can you do to research an active haunting? Small communities may not have a historical society, but they may have a local historian. Ask around, but don't be discouraged if no name comes up. The local newspaper or library may be able to give contact information for the local historian, who is often an amateur history buff or a retired history professor.

Running an ad in the local newspaper or posting a query in message boards for the area may turn up leads to events in the past. It doesn't have to be a large ad or even refer to ghosts directly. You merely need to say you want to talk to someone who has knowledge of a particular address at a particular time.

Neighbors and former neighbors are often happy to come forward to tell you what they have heard about a haunted location. Sometimes they will know how to reach former occupants of the house who may have experienced something during their time at the property.

These days, people seem more accepting of the paranormal. In fact, many people are actually eager to speak of their experiences. Interviews with these people should be conducted with the same care and courtesy as those with the primary residents who called you in.

If you speak with a former neighbor who hasn't lived nearby in some years, remember that his memory may be hazy. People may not remember the details or may make things up to fill in the gaps. The information obviously isn't as fresh as that you obtain from more recent residents or neighbors, but you may get enough information to draw some parallels between the older reports and the newer ones.

If any of the witnesses have children, be discreet around them. Talk of ghosts and hauntings can be quite scary for children, and they should be sent out of the room before you begin the interview.

Occasionally, neighbors or former residents will want to know what is going on and why you are investigating. Discuss this possibility with your client before you cast a wide net to interview others. The client may not want any publicity and may not want anyone else to be brought into the case. Always honor your client's wishes regarding confidentiality. Clients who don't put any restrictions on the investigation may find that by not limiting the research they are giving themselves a better chance of resolving the case satisfactorily. However, while finding the history is important, it may not actually be relevant to the case you're investigating. Do not assume that connections exist until the facts support it.

68. Basic Forms for Investigations

There are two basic types of forms—those you use when dealing with clients and those you use within your organization to record observations, information, and evidence.

Forms for use when dealing with clients include those that will help protect you and your client from liability. Other forms simply spell out the procedures and clarify gray areas. As groups gain experience, they may feel the need to revise or change their basic forms.

A good form covers you legally and reassures clients that they are in the hands of pros looking out for their best interests. Clients in museums, historic houses, or homes with expensive furnishings appreciate knowing that your team will responsibly handle furnishings and infrastructure.

Your client may fear being gossiped about or ridiculed in the community. If that's the case, reassure him that the confidentiality agreement means all of his information will remain secret. He may also worry that his home will be damaged if he lets a bunch of strangers run loose in it. Part of any agreement between the client and the investigators should cover what behavior is expected of the team as they conduct the investigation. If the client wants to add something to the contract specifying that personal items may not be touched or duct tape will not be used in certain locations, the client's agreement should contain these requests.

You can make these forms yourself if you're handy on the computer. If you aren't, search for templates on the Internet. Be sure to have a copy for the client and a copy for the group. All parties to the agreements should sign both.

CLIENT FORMS

+ Client Questionnaire (filled out by the client at or before the initial interview concerning their experiences)
+ Permission to Investigate (signed by the client, allowing the investigators permission to access the property for investigative purposes)
+ Client Interview (to record notes taken during the interview, and answers to set questions)
+ Client Confidentiality Agreement (to assure the client's privacy)
+ Evidence Release or No Release (signed by the client to allow or disallow sharing details of the case)
+ Client Summary Report (given to the client after the investigation and analysis)
+ Follow-Up Questionnaire (filled in by the client after the investigation has taken place)

INTERNAL ORGANIZATION FORMS

+ Investigation Report (a record of the on-site investigation)
+ Location History (see sections 65–67)
+ Incident Report (individual record of any incident that occurs during an investigation)
+ Activity Log (a record of each investigator's activity during the investigation; think of it as a time log as well as a specific record of that each investigator is engaged in)
+ Investigator's Private Report (a personal summary from each investigator regarding their experiences and the investigation overall)
+ Evidence Review Findings (a copy of the data analysis reports)

69. Permission and Release Forms

Two of the most important forms, permission and release forms, deserve a section of their own. A permission form is perhaps the most commonly used instrument for gaining access to a site and protecting the group from future liability. There is no way to legally conduct an investigation without it, and those who do so are setting themselves up for a lot of trouble. Without this basic form, investigators can be arrested and charged with trespassing or perhaps breaking and entering, even if the client initially approached them. This is a little like buying insurance. If the client later alleges the group did not have permission to enter the premises or did damage to it, having the permission form and dated photos of the site can save you from a lawsuit or worse. It is a good idea to have an attorney draw up a simple, legally binding form that spells out the rights and obligations of both parties. Make sure this form has the date, the physical address of the site, and a statement granting the group or researchers access to the premises. It should also include a reassurance from the group that the property will be left as it was found. Add a check box to be ticked and initialed when the key is returned.

In addition to a permission form, you'll want to have the client sign two kinds of release forms:

1. Permission to release confidential information. This release gives the investigators permission to publish information concerning the case. It should clearly state how the information will be used (e.g., put on the group's website, included in a press release, written about in a book, etc.). The release form should offer the client the option of declining permission. In that case, the investigators are bound to protect the client's confidentiality.

2. Release from liability. This form protects both the client and the investigators from any claims arising from the investigation.

Release forms help both sides of the investigation feel comfortable with each other and ensure that neither side is leaving itself open to damage.

Be sure that each permission and release form is signed by the investigators and the client, and that an original of each is kept with the case file.

If a client is reluctant to fill out paperwork, go over it with him and make sure he understands it. Answer any questions. Make it clear that the investigation cannot proceed without it and that signing the paperwork will only take a few minutes.

70. Securing Permission to Access a Site

It can't be emphasized strongly enough: Access to most sites must be obtained and permission granted before investigators traipse around a property. It is just good sense, and it protects the team from annoying and possibly expensive legal issues. If a site is on private property, it is privately owned. Graveyards and cemeteries can be either privately or publicly owned, but police and security patrols may question your presence, especially after dark. They are concerned about potential vandalism.

Always bring along personal identification and a driver's license when taking part in an investigation. Some sort of business card with the name of the group will also enhance your credibility and professional appearance.

Follow these guidelines:

+ Dress normally. Capes, over-the-top costumes, or anything that makes you appear less than professional works against you when you are trying to gain access to a site.

- If you are asked to leave an area, do so immediately. Don't argue or make a scene.
- Never go out alone. Isolated locations can be dangerous. Always bring a cell phone.

Many rookie investigators are stopped cold by the threat of trespassing and feel that it thwarts them from pursuing many kinds of investigations. All it really means is that you should protect your own interests by covering your assets. You can be sued or arrested if you aren't cautious.

Usually, obtaining permission to investigate a location is not hard; in fact, clients who call you almost always automatically give you permission. Be sure to have a permission form prepared for them to sign. The lead investigator should always keep this form with her when on-site.

Even if a building appears vacant, it's important to do your best to track down the owner. Vacant properties may be seasonal residences or vacation homes that are only occupied for part of the year. Alternatively, a vacant property may be temporarily empty while it is being renovated or put on the market for sale. If an owner recently passed away, the home may be caught up in the process of probate. Check the exterior of the property for signs. If the house is for rent or sale, look for a Realtor's sign on the property. There are three other places to do a quick check:

- *Neighbors.* If there are any nearby, they may know the homeowner's name and have her contact information as well. A close neighbor may even have a key and be able to give you permission to enter.

+ *Homeowners' associations.* Subdivisions and gated communities usually have a homeowners' association. They have a list of homeowners and contact information.

+ *The police.* In isolated locations and small towns, the police are a great source of information. They may actually recommend new sites to investigate; they are, after all, in the best position to experience the paranormal if they are called to a location and experience anomalous phenomena. Homeowners who are away will often notify local law enforcement that they are out of town, so the police have their contact information or can direct you to the caretaker.

Some of these approaches will also work for commercial buildings. Ask neighboring businesses; they may share a landlord or know the owner. Ask the police; they are probably aware of who owns the building because they watch abandoned areas to keep an eye out for vandals.

Other information sources include:

+ *City directories.* Sometimes called reverse directories, these large books list who occupies premises. If you have the address, you can find who last occupied the premises. Most public libraries allow you to reference them.

+ *Courthouses and city halls.* Public records are accessible here. Be prepared to pay a small fee in some cases.

Property records, tax records, and probate records can yield the information you seek. The courthouse is the place to obtain property maps and do a title search. The maps are at the county assessor's office, and both the deeds and titles will be available through the county clerk's office. A title search, which shows the records for who owned the house over the years, will reveal the owner's name.

+ *The Internet.* Online resources have grown in recent years. Some towns have their tax assessment records online, and knowing the address is all you need to find the owner. Older homes and businesses may be listed in the National Register of Historical Places, online at *www.nps.gov/nr/.*

It's possible to exhaust your resources and still turn up nothing. Total dead ends are uncommon when the research is thorough, but they do happen and you learn to simply move on. If you cannot track down the owner, put the idea of doing an investigation on the back burner until you can find him and get his consent.

Locating the owner is the first step; getting her permission to enter is the next hurdle. If her property is really haunted, the owner may be defensive about it and may not want to discuss it. This is where a confidentiality agreement and some gentle persuasion will help. Remind her that the information about the investigation is under her control, and if you find that something unusual is going on you may be able to clear the space for her.

What if the owner refuses to give her consent? This happens far less often than you would imagine. Usually, when the benefits of the investigation are explained and the proper forms signed, the owner is glad to grant permission. If she won't, the investigation simply stalls.

Initially, the homeowner or landlord should accompany investigators to the site to open it and remain with them while a walk-through or initial research is done. This shows the proprietor the current state of the property and protects the investigators. If the owner hasn't been to the site in a while, she may be unaware of its true condition and any recent vandalism. Pictures taken at this initial walk-through will document the condition of the property and can prove invaluable if there is any later contention about group liability for any property damage.

Should the owner decline to go or be unable to accompany you, be sure to have her sign your permission and release forms before entering the site.

Even if you secure an owner's or client's permission to access the site, people have been known to change their minds in the middle of an investigation and withdraw their permission to investigate. This is frustrating, but stay calm and try to remedy whatever concern the client has to save the situation and your investment of time and effort. The client does have the right to withdraw permission at any time, and arguing won't help anything. If you can't salvage the situation, exit gracefully with thanks for the client's time, and chalk your findings to date up to experience.

71. Permission-Free Sites

Where can you go to practice and hone your ghost-hunting skills without obtaining permission? Try public places with free access during the daytime—for example, parks, museums, and historic sites. If you enter these areas after dark, you should notify the proper people or agencies. This may mean alerting the police to the fact that you will be at the location and taking photos. This will save you time and hassles. You can also find out if friends or family will open their homes to you for training. Be careful if you are investigating in the homes of friends or relatives. Be very considerate of their privacy, and be aware of the consequences if you actually turn up something disturbing. Elderly relatives or friends in poor health are not good candidates, as investigations can be stressful for them, particularly if you do discover something.

Another option is a haunted hotel or bed and breakfast. You have permission to be there by virtue of the fact that you have reserved a room, but be discreet if you are investigating in public areas. Ask the management if it is all right to take a few photos; they may be very cooperative. Sometimes they will even tell you where activity has taken place and tell stories of their own personal encounters.

72. Medical Information and Preparedness

Be prepared in the case of a medical emergency during an investigation. Every team leader wants to make sure that no one gets hurt on her watch. You must have a plan to deal with the situation quickly and effectively should someone get hurt or fall ill.

Most groups ask that their staff keep information about their medications, medical conditions, doctors, and emergency contacts up to date and on file in a sealed envelope. These envelopes are taken on investigations in case a medical emergency arises and someone needs treatment.

Carefully consider how stressful it might be to meet up with something unexpected during an overnight vigil in a cold, dark house. Being a paranormal investigator is not for the faint of heart, nor is it for you if you have:

+ Heart problems
+ High blood pressure
+ Risk of stroke
+ Diabetes
+ Asthma
+ Any chronic, debilitating illness

Investigators with existing medical conditions should be sure they have adequate medication with them to complete the investigation and that they have informed the team leader of these conditions.

Carrying a first-aid kit is a must. The longer you traipse around dark houses in the middle of the night, the more likely you are to end up with a boo-boo or two. Sometimes investigators in the field are twenty miles from the nearest town and they have only themselves and their fellow investigators to count on if an emergency arises. Emergencies can be caused by the psychological or physical stress of the investigation or by an accident that happens on the scene. Bring a first-aid kit on every investigation as a matter of course. The first-aid kit should contain the following items:

- Band-Aids and bandages
- Aspirin and Tylenol
- Antiseptics
- Anti-itch cream
- Water

If a site investigation was done beforehand, investigators will know of any hazards in the environment, which can range from asbestos contamination to the possibility of snakebite—both unlikely. If someone on your team is bitten by something poisonous, bring its body to the emergency room, if possible, so it can be identified and the proper treatment administered.

Some groups keep epinephrine in the first-aid kit. Anaphylactic shock can occur if an airway becomes obstructed due to bee stings or other shock reactions. Epinephrine keeps the airway from closing completely and can save someone's life until you can get him to an emergency room.

If at all possible, park as near to the site as you can. In case of emergency, you can get to a vehicle and to a hospital much faster.

Most groups now insist that members sign a medical consent form disclosing any treatment they are undergoing and listing any prescriptions they are taking and conditions that might cause problems in the course of an investigation. A separate form releases the organization from liability in the event the person is injured during the investigation.

SAMPLE RELEASE FORM

I, the undersigned, agree to release _____

_____ ,

its members, and their families of my own free will from any and all responsibility for any and all damage that may occur to me and my personal property during the course of the investigation. I furthermore and of my own free will release ____

_____ ,

its members, and their families of any and all responsibility whatsoever for any physical or psychological harm that may at any time come to me as a result of attending and observing an investigation involving paranormal phenomena.

I acknowledge and understand that _____

_____

will not in any way be held responsible for any medical or hospital costs associated with injuries or illnesses I may sustain in the course of the investigation.

In signing this release, I acknowledge that I waive liability and will hold _____

_____ harmless for any injury arising from my participation.

I have read this agreement, understand it, and sign it voluntarily as my own free act and deed; no oral representations, statements, or inducements, apart from the foregoing written agreement, have been made.

I am at least eighteen (18) years of age and fully competent; and I execute this release for full, adequate, and complete consideration fully intending to be bound by same.

Signature: _____

Date: _____

Witness: _____

Date: _____

You may wish to have the signature witnessed by a notary. Organizations that do not ask observers and participants in an investigation to sign such forms are putting themselves at grave legal risk. If the parties involved are minors, their parents or guardians must sign the release form.

73. Getting Insurance and Covering Your Assets

Ghost hunting is risky business, and it doesn't hurt to have some insurance coverage. If you have a small group, individual members can carry their own coverage. Make sure they insure their own individual equipment as well.

Talk with your insurance agent about full replacement cost insurance to cover the equipment. Make sure the policy covers your equipment whether it is taken on an investigation, left in the car, or stored at your home.

The cost of replacing equipment isn't cheap. If the technology gets fried and suddenly stops working during an investigation, a little extra insurance coverage will seem like a very good idea indeed. You can purchase the insurance through an insurance agency; there is no need to disclose that it will be used on ghost hunts, though you will need to explain that it may be taken off-site.

Part 8
GEAR AND TECHNOLOGY

Good observational skills, accurate recording of information, and an inquiring (yet skeptical) mind are prerequisites for ghost hunting that will probably never change. But to capture verifiable evidence, a set of good equipment is invaluable to a paranormal researcher.

To build your ghost-hunting toolbox, acquire equipment as your budget allows and keep an eye on it when you're in the field. You should keep your investment in equipment to a minimum until you are sure your interest in the paranormal will continue. Investigators have shown significant results with less expensive equipment, so don't let the cost of the more expensive items discourage you.

74. Ghost Hunting in the Digital Age

A host of digital aids are available to the paranormal investigator. Digital photography is now readily accessible to almost everyone. The new generation of audio software can be loaded onto home computer systems and can filter out background noises and boost weak audio signals, allowing paranormal investigators to more easily analyze audio data captured on both analog and digital recorders. Digital thermometers, too, have increased in sophistication. They are more sensitive than ever to slight temperature fluctuations and the movement of cold spots. Electromagnetic field (EMF) meters are easier to use and more sensitive, with lights that alert users to readings beyond normal ranges.

A DVR, digital camera, or tape recorder should be in use at all times as you work. It's best to use at least two of the three at all times. They will provide you with valuable data to be analyzed and verified.

75. Paranormal Investigation Gear

The most important paranormal investigative gear you will ever use is your own common sense and judgment. However, for those who are determined to approach the field of ghost hunting in a scientific way, commercial markets and Internet stores are loaded with specialized devices that can help you detect and document paranormal phenomena. Although many researchers say poltergeists are notoriously difficult to capture using the new technologies, even their shenanigans can sometimes be captured with video cameras.

A WORD OF CAUTION

Equipment frequently malfunctions at certain allegedly haunted locations. Batteries drain, monitors go dead, and all sorts of equipment problems occur. When equipment is removed from the site, its functionality usually returns. Many paranormal researchers believe that solar activity also has an effect on electronic equipment (and even on ghosts themselves). Geomagnetic field disturbances may damage power systems, cause false readings, or even give a boost of energy to spirit manifestations and interactions.

You do not need all the gadgets listed in this book to carry out a paranormal investigation. Individuals who are into ghost hunting as a hobby and are not into the advanced research and investigation aspect of it can begin their investigations with as little as a light source, a compass, a voice recorder, and a camera.

In later chapters, more sophisticated equipment is described. In addition, you may wish to carry:

+ Dust masks
+ Laptop computer
+ Mini strobe light (a strobe light makes quick movement seem slower than it is)
+ Facial-composite software program (this can help you construct a potential image of a face from description or memory)

Should you decide to shop online, check out *www.ghostvillage* *.com* or *http://theghosthunterstore.net.*

76. Video and Still Photography

A picture is worth a thousand words. That's never more true than when it comes to pictures of the paranormal. Since digital photos are easily manipulated, people tend to be suspicious of all images in general and ghost photos in particular, but it is still truly stunning to see video or still photos of apparitions or ghosts.

A controversy rages in the paranormal community over the use of digital photography. Researcher Troy Taylor argues that digital camera images of more than five megapixels have sufficient resolution and clarity for investigators to use them. The technology has evolved, and newer models are no longer plagued by problems with false orbs. Some models also offer other important features, such as a nightshot mode.

Digital photo files have vital information embedded within them. They can tell you about the camera make and model, the date and time the image was shot, what camera settings were used, whether flash was used, and the ISO settings. If an attempt is made to manipulate the image, the embedded data records this information as well. You can easily analyze a digital image to see if it has been manipulated.

More expensive digital cameras offer a format known as *raw*. These files are uncompressed. Any anomalous raw image that is examined using this format can be easily authenticated.

According to paranormal investigator Kenneth Biddle, digital cameras with flashes often give the photographer a false positive result. Items with reflective qualities such as brass, chrome, silverware, and even highly polished wood will return a reflection if a flash is used. "If the surface is close enough," says Biddle, "you get an 'apparition' in your photograph."

Investigators still use regular film cameras as well, but the photos are usually scanned into a computer database for easy file storage, enhancement, and transfer. Physical photos and negatives can be labeled and stored in binders for easy access in the office.

77. Audio Voice Recorders and Electronic Voice Phenomena

Small devices that pack lots of investigative punch, recorders can be extremely useful and inexpensive investigative tools for ghost hunters. The technology is advancing quickly, so check online stores frequently to see if prices have dropped or capabilities have grown.

The sound quality of digital recorders is excellent and digital files are easily copied and transferred.

TESLA AND USING AUDIO EQUIPMENT TO SEE OTHER WORLDS

The idea of audio equipment being able to access another world is hardly new. Nikola Tesla (1856–1943) was an electronics genius whose early radio receivers picked up organized, intelligent signals during a time when the only functioning radio transmitter was Guglielmo Marconi's. Tesla studied the phantom signals and speculated they might originate from another planet—or even the spirit world. There were claims that he invented a Teslascope for the purpose of communicating with spirits or extraterrestrials.

Tape and digital voice recorders are used in paranormal investigations to tape interviews with witnesses and to record voice messages from the spirit world. Electronic voice phenomena (EVP) are of particular use to serious investigators. EVPs are unexplained audio events that can sometimes be heard as they are happening, but more often go unheard until the recording is played back during evidence review.

The EVP voices on the recordings are often distinctive, talking in regional accents and dialects. Some seem to struggle to get the words out, as if they are communicating over vast distances. They often call researchers by name. Some may even answer questions or queries about their names or history. That sort of exchange is very exciting for investigators, particularly if they can substantiate some of the information.

A phenomena related to EVP is known as PCFTD—phone calls from the dead. For decades, people have reported receiving telephone calls from deceased family members and friends. Many of the reports are similar—a person receives a phone call late at night, and although the connection is bad, they can recognize the caller's voice. When the recipient of the call makes a reference to the person being dead, the call abruptly ends.

There are three types of audio recording devices commonly used in investigations:

- *Microcassettes.* These small analog recorders have micro audiotapes. If you currently have one, you probably don't have to replace it with a digital recorder. If you're considering it, beware: the less expensive digital recorders sometimes don't have a function that allows their data to be transferred to a computer or other storage device, whereas you can store a microcassette on its own and access it whenever you need to by popping it into the recorder. Some microcassette recorders can be hooked up to a computer via audio cables and the recording transferred in real time to a program such as Audacity if you want to try to clean up the sound. Always keep the original recording, however, as proof.
- *Digital voice recorders.* Tiny and inconspicuous with no tape, these digital recorders have great sound quality. Files from DVRs can be uploaded to computers for analysis and audio cleanup. Files can also be e-mailed or posted on websites.
- *Wireless microphones.* An often-overlooked tool for paranormal research, these devices are growing in popularity. The wireless microphone allows users to record audio

straight to the hard drive of a computer, virtually eliminating background noise. Most kits include a microphone, transmitter, and receiver.

78. Thermometers and Chilly Spirits

Cold spots and sudden temperature fluctuations are of major
interest to investigators. One hypothesis is that when there
is a sudden drop of temperature in a given area, something
is drawing energy in an attempt to manifest. For that reason,
researchers like to measure temperature and temperature
changes during paranormal investigations. These three devices
are commonly used:

+ *Remote sensor wireless thermometer*. The device should be
  placed in a remote area that needs to be monitored. It
  shows temperature changes and will alert investigators if
  there is a sudden shift in temperature.
+ *Infrared thermometer*. This is a pistol-grip meter,
  equipped with a laser pointer, that will measure tem-
  peratures from 0°F to 600°F from a safe distance. It is
  incredibly accurate and has a backlit LCD readout for
  ease of use in dim lighting conditions. It can be used to
  quickly measure the temperature of corridors, rooms,
  basements, or attics.
+ *Hardwire thermometer*. This is a high-tech thermometer
  used primarily to back up readings found with infrared
  thermometers. They use an extremely sensitive wire

probe, which is hard-wired into an equally sensitive meter with a digital readout. The probe is then placed in the target area to record the temperature.

79. Infrared and Thermal Imaging Cameras

Infrared light is electromagnetic radiation with wave lengths beyond the visible spectrum. This technology may hold the key to getting results during an investigation. However, some ghost hunters scoff at this notion, believing it is better to see and record in the full spectrum of light, rather than limiting yourself to just part of the spectrum. When triggered by an infrared motion sensor, a security camera in Sydney, Australia, taped a glowing, vaporous apparition moving along a stairway. Although some skeptics have dismissed it as a cobweb, others claim it shows an object solid enough to have registered on the camera's motion detector.

Prices vary depending on the features you want, but night-vision video cameras, which use infrared technology, are not too expensive and have all the bells and whistles a paranormal investigator would need.

Readily available and cheaply purchased, infrared motion detectors can detect anomalies in a controlled area in two ways:

1. The device's passive infrared motion detector sweeps the zone and compares the area's thermal makeup to the reading it took upon activation.

2. The device's infrasonics detect noise in the sweep area and any sudden disturbance in the room's air mass. Small objects, even on the molecular level, will displace enough air within the room to trip a warning signal.

Thermal imaging cameras, which are a type of infrared technology, are proving to be a very interesting resource for investigators. These cameras, which measure heat signatures, can be used to record interviews as well as the actual course of the investigation.

In one instance of thermal imagery, paranormal researchers Jason Hawes and Grant Wilson captured a full-body apparition standing a few feet away from them in a sanatorium. The apparition was invisible to the naked eye yet showed very clearly in the view screen of the thermal imager.

80. EMF and ELF Meters

Intense emotional events, such as a murder, suicide, or the tragic loss of a loved one, might leave an electrical imprint on the surrounding area. The human brain constantly releases small electrical discharges that may be powerful enough to imprint themselves onto objects in the immediate area. These imprints can be detected by electronic devices.

Electromagnetic frequency (EMF) and extremely low frequency (ELF) meters are widely used by ghost hunters today because they can be so helpful in finding paranormal activity.

However, they all require a certain amount of familiarization and training. Remember that any equipment, no matter what model or brand, can give a false reading in the presence of the following:

+ Poorly grounded or unshielded structural wiring
+ Microwave ovens in use
+ Dimmer switches
+ Cellular phones in use
+ FM, FRS, GRS, and CB radio transceivers in use
+ Air conditioning and power system/stations
+ Television screens, plasma screens, and LCD screens
+ Computers
+ Power lines within 100 yards, especially high voltage (tension) towers and transformers
+ Fuse boxes

As in other fields of serious scientific study, one tool may be better suited for a situation than another.

+ *K2 EMF meters* have five LED lights that alert the user to different levels of electromagnetic field activity. These lights make using the meter in the dark a whole lot easier. The ghost hunting theory about EMF activity is that manmade EMF will stay steady, while paranormal activity will produce peaks and spikes in the reading, because spirits emit a pulsing electromagnetic field. As soon as the meter goes to the second light, it is a definite indication of a higher than normal level of electromagnetic energy. We know that electromagnetic fields are always around us. This meter compensates for this ambient field and will only give an alert when the field is above the human threshold or is significantly higher than normal. Manifesting entities will typically cause the meter to go all the way up to the highest level and make the meter readings spike. That's pretty exciting to witness.

+ Use a *gauss meter* when sensitivity, ultra-fast reactivity, wide detection range, and audible tones are needed on an investigation. A gauss is a unit of measurement of a magnetic field, named after German mathematician and physicist Karl Friedrich Gauss. They are precision instruments designed for specific situations. A single-axis gauss meter detects paranormal activity within an area by showing the "electromagnetic smog signature" such activity generates. These instruments are very accurate and fast. A color-coded graph indicates the level of a field's intensity at a glance.

+ The moderately priced *gauss multi-detector* also detects magnetic fields. It measures values in both electrostatic and electromagnetic scales independently and with high accuracy. Using a corresponding colored bank of LED lights and a field-strength rating capability ranging from .00001 to 1.0 on both the electrostatic and electromagnetic scales, this device is a necessity for most serious investigators. Some models come with a built-in audible signal feature as well.

+ An *EMF/gauss meter* or *ELF meter* detects electro-static (Tesla) and electromagnetic (gauss) fields with extremely high sensitivity, and it has a very high range and accuracy of measurement. A frequency filter allows different frequency fields to be monitored separately, so both VLF/RF (very low frequency/radio frequency) and ELF can be measured. It features lights that give the user the ability to read results in dark areas. Both the RF and gauss meter portion provide audible sound and large flashing lights, which correspond to abnormal spikes in field strength.

+ A *TriField Natural EM meter* is relatively expensive, sensitive, and easily damaged, so they are not feasible for many paranormal investigators. Designed to detect only what we would consider paranormal activity, they take most of the guesswork out of situations where the gauss, ELF, and ion detectors may leave investigators otherwise unsure of their findings. They are fairly sim-ple to use and have the audible warning tone so neces-sary in dark areas.

As this field matures, ghost hunters have learned more and more about the limits of the technology used in investi-gations. Teams using the TriField Natural EM Meter discov-ered recently that this meter is so sensitive it can be affected by lightning within seven miles of the site. Investigators now have to double-check weather reports before going on an investiga-tion to ensure they aren't getting bad readings. It is extremely important to learn as much as possible about environmental conditions before gathering evidence.

During the course of a professional investigation, good record keeping and cross-referencing information by each individual team member gives perspective and depth. If technology is used, the data from the equipment must be carefully recorded for analysis later.

81. Low-Tech Tools: Flashlights, Lanterns, Compasses, and Watches

People sometimes underestimate simple, low-tech tools. If you have a limited budget, some of these devices can replace their high-price counterparts in the short term. Sometimes batteries drain and electronic devices fail; when that happens, even those who have the high-tech gear may be glad they brought along backup.

Flashlights are an essential, basic item for any investigator. Naturally, most investigations occur after dark, and when it is time to cut off power, the flashlight becomes one of the few light sources available. The investigator should have a red filter fitted to the lens or a red bulb. The red-tinted light keeps night vision intact and eyes adjusted to lower light levels. Lots of extra batteries are also essential.

Flashlights have their place, but batteries can drain quickly and it is good to have backup. Kerosene *lanterns* can provide light when flashlights die, and although they are more cumbersome and expensive than the average flashlight, they can be enormously helpful.

Simple in both its construction and function, the *compass* is probably the most overlooked yet dependable paranormal tool in existence. The humble compass is a highly dependable electromagnetic field sensor. It has largely been replaced by more accurate and sensitive electronics, but this paranormal tool is still used by many investigation traditionalists and those who wish to have a dependable backup to their modern-day electronic equipment. Compass needles can be moved by entities with a strong EMF that may well be paranormal in origin.

A reliable *watch* is an essential bit of equipment for keeping track of time spent during the investigation and to help coordinate the team's efforts. Consider an analog watch as well as a digital timepiece.

82. Miscellaneous Other Equipment

You may find other equipment helpful in your investigations. Some of this equipment is quite costly, and only big-budget investigators can afford it. In some cases, cheaper equipment can duplicate its functions.

+ A *thermal imager* is designed so the user can easily see and then analyze heat signatures and remnant heat signatures. It analyzes hot and cold atmospheric anomalies instantly. This sophisticated tool is extremely expensive.

◆ A *magnetic field sensor* can detect, monitor, and document even the slightest change in a magnetic field through computer software enhancement. The Rhode Island Paranormal Research Group (T.R.I.P.R.G.) has used this device to successfully confirm the presence of entities when its sensitives are trying to communicate with them. These magnetic field sensors are so sensitive they can detect even the slightest shift in Earth's gravitational fields.

◆ A *digital thermal hygrometer* is an invaluable tool to record temperature and humidity data. Investigators say it is worth its weight in gold, particularly when investigating orb activity and determining whether an orb is natural or paranormal.

◆ The *air ion counter* is used for the detection of both positive and negative natural and artificial ions. It is standard paranormal theory that when a ghost/spirit is about to manifest, a certain amount of energy is drawn from the surrounding environment or from nearby sources. An air ion counter measures the resulting change in the positive or negative ions (electrostatic energy) in the air. It is a fascinating tool in the paranormal investigator's arsenal.

◆ A set of *two-way radios* or other handheld communication is an absolute must for responsible and safe paranormal investigations. Groups that are spread out over a large area need to maintain communication with all members at all times to ensure their safety during investigations and to coordinate their efforts. These handy little devices make that possible. Most of today's handheld transceivers have a two-to-five-mile range and are powerful enough to transmit through walls and obstacles to allow clear communications in all kinds of weather.

+ If you're serious about your research, a *Geiger counter*, a meter formally associated with atom bombs and radiation, may be a good idea. These meters are tough, durable, portable, and powerful. They're also very affordable. Paranormal energy ionizes the air and this meter instantly detects changes in the number of negatively and positively charged ions.

+ A monitoring system such as a *closed-circuit TV* with night-vision capability allows an investigative team to monitor one or more areas simultaneously without risking direct exposure to any paranormal activity. Unfortunately, its cost usually puts it out of reach of most groups. If there is suspicion of the presence of inhuman entities or poltergeists, investigators may find this system well worth the cost.

+ If you have plenty of cash to throw into your gear, quality *night-vision devices* are durable and incredibly useful. They eliminate the need for flashlights and enable investigators to travel through completely lightless areas in total safely. Military surplus stores are a good source for this sort of equipment.

+ Enhanced *sound-level meters* are widely available on the Internet through specialty stores and merchants. They are used in paranormal investigation to detect ELF (extra-low-frequency) and EHF (extra-high-frequency) sounds. With slight modification, such a meter will easily pick up the sound of a tape recorder in operation, or a video camera's mechanical signature. If hoaxsters have set up equipment in a building to try to trick investigators, this device will help find that equipment by locating the sound of it in operation. Since it is so sensitive, a sound-level meter is extremely useful to the EVP-seeking investigator and very helpful when determining the quietest location to place microphones and recording devices.

* Inexpensive and portable, *black light* or *UV light* is an interesting multiuse tool for investigators. It can be used to detect airborne particles in a room or building, and it also allows investigators to distinguish between true orb phenomena and nonparanormal airborne contaminants. Some paranormal investigators theorize that you can use a black light to "push" spirits out of an area and herd them toward another space, where they can then, perhaps, be photographed or contacted. Many of these very affordable devices also come with a flashlight feature.

83. Practical Clothing

Most ghost hunters talk about the benefits of layering and wearing thermal underwear on hunts during the colder months. It is important to be practical. You'll be out late at night, in the dark, often without heat of any kind. Comfort and protection from the elements become very big priorities during overnight hunts. Comfortable shoes or sneakers are a must, too. Apart from weather-appropriate clothing, make sure your team wears practical, site-specific clothing.

Make sure you have clothing with lots of pockets to stash your ghost-hunting paraphernalia. Many researchers wear fishing vests, but now you can actually find online stores that sell clothing designed for ghost hunters. Don't forget to protect your gear from the weather, as well.

Juggling your gear and equipment can be a challenge. With a K2 meter in one hand, an audio recorder in the other, and a camera around your neck, it may be a struggle to scribble your notes during the investigation. Lots of investigators jot down as much info as they can initially and then take a break every fifteen to thirty minutes to record what has happened in the interim. You can also hang a small digital audio recorder from a cord around your neck to free up your hands. Most have a simple switch that can turn on the recorder, allowing quick dictation about the conditions, equipment readings, and impressions of the location, and some even have a voice-activated recording function. Sometimes, investigators actually capture EVP during this process—talk about multitasking! A belt with pouches or hooks for various equipment can be useful, too.

84. Capturing Electronic Voice Phenomena

One of the most exciting developments in the field of psychic exploration is the use of technology to capture unexplained human voices or sounds electronic voice phenomena, or EVP.

EVPs were first discovered quite by accident by Friedrich Jürgenson as he was recording birdcalls near his home in Sweden during the 1950s. He was flabbergasted when he heard a man's voice telling him how to better record the bird songs. Totally intrigued, Jürgenson continued his recordings for many years after that and subsequently published a book, *Voices From the Universe*, that described his method of electronic communication with the dead.

Some claim the discovery of EVP goes much further back than that. Thomas Edison, the inventor of the telephone, was quoted in *Scientific American* in the 1920s as saying: "Nobody knows whether our personalities pass on to another existence or sphere, but it is possible to construct an apparatus which will be so delicate that if there are personalities in another existence or sphere who wish to get in touch with us in this existence or sphere, this apparatus will at least give them a better opportunity to express themselves than the tilting tables and raps and Ouija boards and mediums and the other crude methods now purported to be the only means of communication."

Anyone can try to capture EVP. It can be done with either analog or digital recorders, though the analog method will probably be phased out very shortly because of the superior quality of digital voice recorders and the ease of transferring files to a computer. Some investigators recommend performing the experiments outside your own home; after all, if something disturbing is discovered it may upset you and change how you feel about your personal living space.

Follow these steps to record an EVP:

1. Prepare the equipment and check to see that the batteries are charged and everything is in good working order.
2. Tune an AM or FM radio to the space between channels to generate white noise. Running water and computer programs that generate background noise will also work.
3. State the date, the time, your name, and where you are at the beginning of the session.
4. Ask a question, and wait about thirty seconds for a response, letting the white noise run softly in the background.
5. Continue asking questions in this way. Ask as many as you like, but remember that you have to review the recording. Keep your sessions short at first; thirty minutes will suffice.
6. Be polite. There is no need to provoke any entity.
7. Transfer your recording onto the hard drive of your computer and play it back. Audio programs can be used to clean up the files and boost the sound.

A staggering number of EVP have been gathered in the last sixty years, and some of them have been clear enough for friends and family to recognize the voices of dead loved ones.

EVP gathered in different regions of Europe not only speak with accents appropriate to the country, but in some instances the voices on these EVP have spoken in ancient forms of German or Italian. They often answer questions put to them in languages no longer spoken today but totally pertinent to the history of the site being investigated.

Maggie Florio, an investigator with The Rhode Island Paranormal Research Group, says of her EVP, "I use a digital voice recorder. Sometimes I carry it around with me and sometimes I place it in an area that is active. I usually ask a few questions like, 'What is your name? Did you live here (work here, play here, etc.)? How old are you? Can you see me? Are you aware that you are no longer on the earthly plane?' I wait about thirty seconds in between questions for any answers that may come. I try not to record longer than one hour, because it is tiresome to review. I sometimes play one section a half dozen times if I think there is an EVP. I write down the time and what I think the EVP says."

Most people who use digital voice recorders upload their files to a computer to tweak the sound quality and boost the signal. Most also use some sort of audio software program to clean up the recording for optimal quality. Florio uses Wavepad and a regular computer microphone to review her tapes. "I don't mess with the EVP very much," she says. "If I can't hear what is being said, I may amplify it to eliminate the hum and hiss, but that's about it."

85. White Noise and the Ghost Box

While doing their EVP work, many investigators like to use some sort of white-noise generator behind the scenes. Why?

White-noise generators are said to give the spirits something to work with, perhaps the raw material out of which to build the sounds later discovered on the recordings. Software that generates this noise can be found for free or on a trial basis on the Internet.

The ongoing work using EVP is one of the most exciting in the field of psychic research. You don't need a lot of fancy equipment to do your own investigations and analysis of your results. You simply need an audio recorder, preferably a digital one, with an external microphone, if possible. To generate white noise, simply tune a radio between stations, or download white-noise generator software from the Internet. To do your analysis and data storage, you will need a computer and audio software.

The latest breakthrough development in EVP phenomena is the so-called *ghost box*. This device is said to greatly increase your chance of recording an EVP. It produces random voltage to create white noise (static) from an AM tuner, which is then amplified, fed into an echo chamber, and recorded. Fans of the device, which scans through live radio frequencies, say it allows spirits to pull the words they want to use from the broadcasts in order to string together a message that can be heard. What sets the ghost box apart from simple EVP devices is that you can hear the response in real time, rather than only after the fact. This could lead to the opportunity for two-way communication with spirits of the departed, a true breakthrough.

The experience, as one report states, is "not unlike chatting with someone by walkie-talkie." A degree of training is required to catch the messages, which are sometimes heavily overlaid with static-filled background noise. But after a bit of experimenting, the responses become increasingly more intelligible, and sentences and answers to questions can be discerned. Voices heard over the ghost box can have a very strange quality to them and may sound mechanical. More often than not, EVP sound like a person speaking, complete with regional accents.

Just as in the realm of mediumship, some entities seem to be in control and act as gatekeepers, bringing other spirits through to communicate. Notably, ghost-box operators in separate locations, distant from one another, have sometimes recorded the same guides or controllers.

Frank Sumption created the original ghost box. You can visit his Yahoo Group, *http://tech.groups.yahoo.com/group/evp-itc/*, to familiarize yourself with the whole ghost-box concept. Keyport Paranormal (*www.keyportparanormal.com*) has information on how to make your own ghost box, with schematics, examples of audio files captured from a ghost box made from a Radio Shack radio, and links to EVP software.

86. Capturing Elusive Images

Now that many people own digital cameras, we are bound to see an upsurge in ghostly images, real or imagined. The furor over orbs in the first few years of digital shooting put many investigators off them forever, but if you are serious about attempting to capture paranormal images, your patience may just pay off. New-model digital cameras do not suffer from the same technical issues that plagued the early models, causing every speck of dust to look like an orb.

The best approach when trying to capture photographic evidence is to keep shooting. Whenever possible, use the room's own available light and turn off the flash. Then, if the image of an orb is captured, no one can protest that it was the flash bouncing off a dust particle or an insect.

When reviewing photos that appear to capture paranormal activity, rule out everyday explanations. For example, is what you're seeing really an anomaly, or is it a natural occurrence? When the investigator took the photo, did he simply not notice that another investigator was in the frame at the time? And, importantly, is it your desire to see something paranormal that is making you see it?

Part 9
TEAMWORK

A team's greatest asset is its faith in a strong alliance with other team members. Team members must know without question that their teammates will always put the team's best interests and well-being before any other consideration, including gathering evidence.

When putting together a team, you should know what kind of professionals are out there and what their fields of expertise are to form a balanced lineup. Unique cases may also yield the need to call on specialists who aren't necessarily regular members of your team.

87. A Team Leader's Accountability to Team Members

Team leaders who organize investigations have a lot more responsibility than the rest of the team. They should have gained confidence in their leadership abilities over time and feel sufficiently motivated before being put in charge of an investigation. A certain level of maturity must be evident, because the team depends on the decisions the team leader makes and they must have implicit faith in her judgment.

Just as the team leader is responsible to the members, the members are responsible to one another, the team leader, and the client. They should never argue with one another while on a case or speak ill of one another to clients or the media. If they have concerns about a fellow member that are pertinent to the case, they should resolve it within the group by requesting a meeting.

If an investigation is characterized by chaos, confusion, and ineptitude, the person in charge of the investigation is going to bear the brunt of the responsibility for it. If he cannot delegate authority and responsibility properly, it will soon become apparent.

Ideally, in larger, better-established organizations, the role of the team leader rotates as cases demand. This role may fall to the older investigators who have been on many cases and know the ropes, but they should be supportive when a novice investigator becomes a team leader for the first time.

The team leader bears the primary responsibility for:

1. Working with the client
2. Conducting an ethical, fair investigation
3. Ensuring fellow team members' safety
4. Supervising personnel and property in a professional manner

While all of these responsibilities are important and inter-connected, client confidentiality and safety issues are paramount.

If a new team member deliberately or inadvertently violates one of the team leader's rules about how to behave on-site or with the client, take him aside and warn him that he has committed an infraction of the rules and should be more aware of his actions. Handle the warning in a low-key and sensitive way. If he argues or proves disruptive, he should be asked to leave the site. Review his membership status as soon as possible.

It can be more serious when a veteran team member violates the rules because for longtime members, these procedures should be ingrained, almost second nature. Again, draw the member away from the investigation and talk with her to discover why the infraction occurred. While there may be a good reason, the team member may have grown sloppy in her approach and needs to have a refresher course in proper protocols.

If necessary, ask the offender to leave the site until the problem can be resolved. Never argue in front of the client and try not to embarrass or humiliate the team member in front of her peers.

88. Two Key Team Positions: Case Manager and Equipment Manager

While every team member is important, some positions are integral to the smooth running of a team, and therefore require special attention.

The case manager organizes and coordinates all the data and files you accumulate in the course of your investigations. The case manager's responsibilities include noting the intake of new cases and managing the data from ongoing investigations. Since the case manager is the first point of contact when a potential client calls the group for help, she must quickly ascertain whether the person is desperate, frantic, in danger, or just curious about paranormal activity. She must be a good judge of human nature, too, as ghost-hunting groups are targeted for more than their fair share of hoaxes.

The case manager's job does not end there; she is in charge of filing and organizing the old cases so their data is accessible to both the organization and the client. It may be a thankless job, but some people love it, because it gives them ready access to case files and the information that they provide.

The case manager is also the person who does background research prior to the actual investigation. She digs out facts and background history and acts as the go-to person for the team regarding basic information and setup. The case manager is the backbone of the team. With the right person in the job, the workflow goes very smoothly and the group functions at its optimal level.

Not all paranormal investigation organizations are fortunate enough to have a dedicated tech person or equipment manager on staff, but those that do find their investigations function much more smoothly. Today's ghost hunts are very technology dependent, and practically all the equipment is innovative technology. The equipment can be bewildering to the nonprofessional; therefore, it makes sense to have at least one team member who can function as the equipment manager, who can figure out where to deploy and how to interface the digital camcorders, electronic field meters, infrared cameras, and motion detectors. This specialized knowledge takes a big responsibility off the shoulders of other team members, who might otherwise waste valuable time and resources trying to figure it all out.

Keeping track of all the equipment and their batteries, cords, and accessories is a daunting task. One person should be responsible for making sure that equipment is field ready and all batteries and accessories are in good working order.

At the end of the investigation, all equipment must be gathered up, checked in, and put away properly. Without a clear division of tasks and responsibilities, things get lost, left behind, or damaged. Most of the equipment is expensive, so it should not be handled carelessly or without the proper training. Remember, investigations can go on for many hours late at night, and everyone is fatigued when the time comes to gather the equipment and pack it away. There should be one person in charge of double checking and supervision of equipment. This ensures all equipment is checked back in efficiently.

89. Reports: Logging a Case from Start to Finish

Team leaders can't be everywhere at once. Only when they read and digest the information from their team's verbal and written reports will they have a comprehensive picture of what actually happened during the investigation. While the investigation is ongoing, they may have some idea of what is happening, but it's often impossible to judge the full impact until all the data has been reviewed.

All members of a paranormal group are involved in record keeping to one degree or another. During the probationary period of training, investigators learn about equipment and procedures, and they are also taught how to interpret and record equipment readings. Each individual investigator logs all the facts and occurrences that might conceivably be of any relevance. There many not be any obvious correlations between the bits of data and evidence, but sometimes it all fits together like a jigsaw puzzle to form a whole, coherent picture.

Most investigations require the use of site-assessment reports and investigation forms. These forms allow the investigators and team leaders to record their experiences on the site in a very organized way. They must include a place to record the following information:

- The investigator's name
- The names of all investigators at the site
- The date, time, and temperature
- The location address
- The equipment in use
- Any unusual events

The personal investigator's log may be included. It can also be a separate form, depending on how much information the team thinks its members should be recording during an investigation. In the personal log, the investigator has more space to write down impressions and personal experiences, which is not always the case in more bare-bones site-assessment and investigation forms.

The site-assessment form and the client report help define the investigation's early days. At various points in the investigation, the team leader usually distills all the data from the various site-investigation forms into one overarching report. She will attempt to identify patterns or determine whether the data indicates a particular course of action. It is the bird's-eye view of the investigation, and it can often point the way to further study of the phenomena and give the team an idea how to proceed.

After an investigation has been completed, the lead investigator or team leader gathers the other investigators' notes and case logs for review. Some groups go so far as to have the logs printed on two- or even three-part forms in order to have a copy for the investigator, the team leader, and the organization's files.

The team leader should go over the written records carefully, looking for anything that may be significant. Information can be derived from crosschecking and comparing the records—for example, did different teams experience the same sort of phenomenon, such as a cold spot or seeing a shadowy figure, at the same location? Did something happen at the same time to all investigators at the site? If so, a further investigation is necessary.

If the lead investigator's review of the written material still leaves gaps in his understanding of the event, he will follow up with any team members whose reports seem incomplete. If an investigator consistently forgets to fill in information that is relevant to the investigation, the team leader needs to emphasize the importance of keeping good, detailed records.

90. Awareness, Responsibility, and Safety

Most teams agree that safety comes first: They should do everything in their power to ensure that no one gets hurt and no accidents or mishaps occur to injure anyone during the investigation. This sort of care and prudence pays off. It builds trust, ensures things will run smoothly, and gives the team pride and a sense of professionalism. What can you do to ensure that the group remains safe on an investigation?

1.   Obtain permission to investigate the site.
2.   Follow proper investigative protocol.

3. Leave if there seems to be a problem regarding your right to be there.

4. Never investigate alone.

5. Bring along adequate equipment and supplies.

6. Bring a first-aid kit.

7. Examine the site for hazards in the daylight prior to a night investigation.

8. Use walkie-talkies or other communication devices to keep team members in touch.

9. Make sure your transportation is reliable and maintain the vehicle(s) used by the team.

10. Have an agreed-upon signal to let members know that it is time to evacuate the premises in an emergency.

11. Bring plastic bags to cover equipment if there is bad weather during an outdoor investigation.

Remember, teammates do not put each other in jeopardy or play pranks that can lead to putting other teammates in danger. This is not to say that investigators can't have any fun during an investigation, but keep in mind that the site is important to someone. It may be someone's home or even place of burial. Act appropriately.

If there are one or more sensitives in the group, pay close attention to them to ensure their safety. They are the most vulnerable to psychic and physical attack and entities are drawn to them more than other investigators. Should they start behaving oddly or seem to be exhausted, they should be taken away from the site before they become ill.

91. Working with Sensitives on the Team

It is generally accepted that certain people, such as psychics, sensitives, and intuitives, have unique access to knowledge through supernatural means. Not all ghost hunters use sensitives in their investigations, but a significant number do. While current trends have investigators relying more on technology than on psychics, that doesn't mean psychics are no longer important in investigations of the paranormal. Their expertise can be valuable on its own; when it is paired with the data gathered by high-tech tools, it can present a well-rounded picture of a haunting.

Teams that include sensitives feel that they are a huge asset to the investigation. Their contributions to the gathering of evidence often prove integral to the case, and they have the ability to bring closure to the restless spirits that created the haunting.

Individuals with different types of psychic abilities might be helpful in the course of an investigation. Different sensitives experience the situation based on their own gifts. For some, the experience is auditory. For others, it is visual. Others may feel a presence, a sensation known as *kinesthesia*.

The sensitives on the case must make a commitment to communicate seamlessly with other members of the team. They must understand that they are not the focus of the team. Their goal must be helping others, so the main thrust of the investigation should always be uncovering the facts and maintaining a high standard of professional behavior. The psychics should be experienced, seasoned investigators in their own right. They should not be prone to melodrama or attention-getting behaviors but should report what they are experiencing as simply and truthfully as possible. They must be adaptable so that no matter what situation arises, they can remain poised and ready to take the appropriate action.

Ideally, sensitives should be trained in normal investigative skills and be able to function as a regular team member, trained to use the equipment and follow proper protocols when need be. It should be obvious to everyone that all jobs on an investigation are of equal importance. Cases are turned on their heads when the investigation revolves entirely around the medium and little verifiable data is gathered. If there is too much emphasis on one area of the investigation, the other aspects suffer as a result.

Some investigators have expressed concern about a phenomenon that sometimes occurs in the presence of very strong psychics, whose perceptions of the spirits or haunting can be so overwhelmingly strong that they can actually help it manifest for onlookers. It is almost as if a very faint signal is boosted by the sensitive's mind. In effect, the observers on scene can influence the outcome of the investigation by their very presence, and more phenomena than usual can be observed. These effects can be a help or a hindrance to the case, depending on the circumstances. They may confuse the team's investigation of the haunting if they are attributed solely to the ghosts.

Many groups have developed procedures and protocols to ensure that any prior access to information about the case is concealed from the psychics and sensitives involved. Most never allow the sensitives to book locations or conduct the preinvestigation interviews. If a sensitive booked the location or even sat in on an interview, it would compromise any future information provided by the psychic or sensitive. It is imperative that the sensitive does not know the facts underlying the case. This could compromise the entire investigation.

Many groups tell the sensitives nothing about the location until they are en route to the site. This protects the sensitive from any appearance of impropriety, especially in the case of famous haunted sites. Maggie Florio of The Rhode Island Paranormal Research Group (T.R.I.P.R.G.) says sensitives in her group are given only the sketchiest idea of where they are going, sometimes only knowing whether they are staying in the area or going farther away. The exact location is divulged after they are already on the road to the site. If the case sensitives do learn any information they shouldn't, they must immediately inform their team leader of it so there will be no issues later. Sensitives know that if they are informed ahead of time about the destination, skeptics could easily make accusations that they had researched information about the site or the case.

Sensitives are also usually isolated during the set-up phase of an investigation, which often means they are left sitting in a vehicle while the equipment is set up and walk-throughs or interviews are done. These steps are not so extreme when you consider that the integrity of the entire investigation may be at stake.

The team's goal is to bring an open and unbiased approach to the case, so it is vital to maintain the utmost integrity. Some groups may even go so far as to cover up anything that may offer clues to the site's history or former occupants—house plaques, grave markers, historical signage, photos, and so on. This is yet another means of making sure the information gleaned by the psychic remains pure, unsullied, and uncontaminated by outside knowledge.

92. Photographers and Videographers

Photographers and videographers are crucial to conducting paranormal investigations. It can be difficult to capture paranormal activity during the day, so the team's photographers and videographers will need to be prepared to shoot at night, either with flash or with night-vision cameras.

Just as with EVP, sometimes when investigators take photos, they don't realize what they've got until they review the material. In this way, digital cameras can be an advantage, because the images can be reviewed while the investigation is still underway. If an anomaly is noted, additional photos can be taken to capture other aspects of it.

+ Take many photos. This helps increase the likelihood of capturing something notable.
+ Avoid taking photos of reflective surfaces (where an everyday explanation, such as the reflection of a flash, can inadvertently be mistaken for paranormal activity).
+ Don't take pictures facing the sun or any bright light. Flares can show up as anomalies.
+ Make sure your lens is clean (to avoid mistaking a smear for a paranormal phenomenon).

◆ If you're taking photos in a cold environment, make sure your breath vapor doesn't show up on the film as a ghostly mist. Same with smoking.

◆ Remove rings, camera wrist straps, and tie back long hair so as not to create false anomalies.

◆ Be sure to bring plenty of batteries (and film, if you're using film).

For more information on ghost photography, visit the website *http://ghoststudy.com/photography_class.html*. It features a step-by-step guide and good tips for would-be ghost photographers. Always remember to be respectful of the rights of others, living and dead, during the shooting process.

93. Parapsychologists and Demonologists

Parapsychologists study paranormal experiences, or experiences that cannot be explained by science. Demonologists study demons and beliefs about demons. While individuals involved in these studies may not be paranormal investigators themselves, they may be valuable contacts upon whom to call for more information regarding your experiences and research.

Ed and Lorraine Warren were parapsychologists and demonologists by trade who became involved in such high-profile cases as the Amityville Horror. It is estimated that from the time they began their work in the 1950s until Ed passed away in 2006, the Warrens investigated more than 4,000 cases. They are considered true pioneers in the field of parapsychology. When the

Warrens first began their paranormal investigations, they were merely trying to help people who needed somewhere to turn when something they could not understand began to disrupt their everyday lives. As demonologists, the Warrens specialized in the phenomenon that surrounds inhuman spirits—demons and devils. Demons—nonhuman, malevolent entities that never walked the earth in human form—are always dangerous. Their intent is never ambiguous; they are out to injure and cause pain by whatever means they find at their disposal.

If you need to locate a parapsychologist, consult the Parapsychological Association at *http://parapsych.org*. You may also be able to find contact information for a parapsychologist or a demonologist at a local metaphysical bookstore.

Part 10

GHOST HUNTING AS A HOBBY OR PROFESSION

Although many people who start out in this field as a hobby eventually find themselves working at it full time, the transition from amateur to professional isn't always easy.

No one-size-fits-all solution exists for making a living as a paranormal investigator. However, unless you are independently wealthy and have the free time to conduct your investigations, you must derive income from some aspect of your work. Every individual must strive to find the correct balance to make it work; no two people will make the same choices.

The best advice is to follow your own instincts and to walk the career path that offers you the most satisfaction. After pursuing the paranormal for a year or so, you will know whether you are ready to make the commitment necessary to do the job full time. Most paranormal investigators truly love their work because it is interesting, challenging, and exciting. Additionally, they derive great satisfaction from rescuing others who are in crisis. Remember, it is possible to help people, whether you are doing it full or part time and whether you're an amateur or a pro.

94. Hobbyist or Professional?

Being an amateur ghost hunter can be a very absorbing pastime. As you explore allegedly haunted sites and learn more and more about the supernatural world, you may find many overlapping areas of interest in related paranormal fields as well.

People who find the study of ghosts fascinating often find themselves drawn to the study of crop circles, extrasensory perception (ESP), psychokinesis (the ability to move objects without touching them), psychometry (the ability to pick up information from objects by merely touching them), and precognition (the ability to predict future events).

In short, you may feel drawn to any of the many types of unexplained phenomena. Lately, there has been an explosion of interest in all of these topics, and you have a wealth of resource material to explore. The Internet is a good place to start your search for information, but keep in mind that much of the data on the web is from unverifiable sources. Used wisely, however, the Internet can provide you with a good general overview of many topics, and you can use bibliographies to steer you toward further research.

The ideal situation for a beginner is to find a group or individual mentor to help you gain the proper experience in the paranormal realm.

Many people ask whether you can actually earn a living as a professional ghost hunter. Unfortunately, the answer is no—certainly not at first. Although paranormal investigating can be very rewarding on a personal level, it is not a particularly lucrative field. The people who go into it do so primarily for unselfish reasons: to help others. You may also find yourself in competition with other ghost-hunting organizations that do not charge for their services.

Realistically, though, not many professional ghost investigators could support themselves without deriving income from some peripheral aspect of their work. Therefore, some may charge an hourly fee or a flat fee for a minimum number of hours. In addition, they supply their client with a written report, photos, and digital videos of the site investigation if any evidence is found. Most, however, find this approach unthinkable and charge no fee whatsoever for their services.

If you're considering going pro, you are probably wondering what entering this field will cost. Credible investigators are usually nonprofit organizations and do not charge for their investigations. Some investigate cases with their own finances or with money collected from donations and sponsors. You might consider making local investigations free of charge, but ask to be reimbursed for hotel costs and travel expenses if you have to travel long distances.

Opinions differ widely among paranormal investigators as to the ethics of allowing clients to reimburse traveling expenses and other costs. Some will not charge a client under any circumstances, while others will only accept payment from an organization and never from an individual.

Although it is true there are few careers that provide the kind of satisfaction that comes from freeing frantic clients from disturbances, you may have to find other ways of supplementing your income.

Here are some ideas:

+ *Teach paranormal classes.* If you are comfortable speaking to groups, you might consider the option of teaching classes on ghosts and paranormal-related subjects. These sessions could be held privately, through a community group, or at a college.
+ *Cleanse spaces.* People increasingly want to clear their homes of any negative energy. Interestingly enough, the real estate laws of many states require full disclosure of paranormal activity when a house is sold, so realtors can be a source of referrals for your services.
+ *Write an article, book, or script.* People with an interest in the paranormal can often build a network once they have established their credentials by writing about the subject. These credentials often lead to other writing assignments.
+ *Work as a media consultant.* Consultation jobs can pay well, and with the growing interest in the paranormal, there are many movies and television shows that will need advice and insight.
+ *Debunk.* Most reports of hauntings turn out to have totally normal explanations. If you as an investigator can alleviate clients' fears and debunk the notion that ghosts are haunting a location, you'll provide a very valuable service.
+ *Maintain a members-only website.* These days, professionals should maintain a site. These sites may have content that is available to the public and a paid membership section as well.

95. Tips on Maintaining a Professional Reputation

Whether you're a pro or a hobbyist, you need to maintain a good reputation. Serious ghost hunters must keep very careful track of the information they uncover during investigations. Lone investigators and organizations alike share the same obligation to the client and the rest of the paranormal community—to keep good records and share nonconfidential data that will lead to a greater understanding of the phenomena observed for *all* researchers in the field. A high standard of professionalism preserves the reputation and the integrity of the group. Here are two tips to help you:

+ *Be organized.* A little organization at the beginning can go a long way toward quickly building a sterling reputation for reliability and professionalism, which are truly invaluable assets to a group of this kind. If you aren't sure you can keep your records organized, partner up with someone who can.
+ *Partner only with responsible team members, and insist on integrity in all areas of an investigation, from start to finish.* Conduct investigations in a professional manner, and let word of mouth spread the good news. Always maintaining professional standards and procedures will quickly allow even new groups to develop a good reputation. This means having group members who are conscientious and considerate in their approach to clients, the property being investigated, and the integrity of the evidence gathered. The whole package has to be there or

word will quickly spread in the community that a group is unreliable. The most important assets an investigator can have are reliability and integrity.

If a team member does not keep good records, for example, she is letting other team members down and effectively sabotaging the investigation. Periodic reviews can help team members stay on track and alert team members to areas they can improve.

How does a ghost-hunting organization build a good relationship with the local community? What are the factors that convince the public that the group is comprised of serious people who are conducting investigations with a measured scientific approach?

+ Be an ongoing presence in the region by maintaining a physical location or office.
+ Work over time to maintain a consistent public profile.
+ Hold educational programs and workshops.
+ Stick to professional protocols and standards.
+ Have members of good character.
+ Offer the organization's services to civic organizations and spread the word about the work.

96. Using Rigorous Methodology

The merits of experiential investigations versus pseudoscientific ones are hotly debated today in paranormal research.

The main thrust of the old school investigation was to prove that something was out there, then to try to find evidence to support it. Secondarily, the goal was to calm the disturbance caused by the paranormal events and to help the client achieve peace of mind. Another objective was to help the entity successfully cross over to the other side. However, the experiential, old-school type of investigation has come to be viewed as totally passé. Perhaps it was the influence of shows like *Ghost Hunters*, but the field became dominated by the scientific approach, where the main thrust of the investigation is to debunk the haunting through the use of scientific equipment.

A strong dose of healthy skepticism is a good place for any investigator of the paranormal to start. If you don't try to debunk potential paranormal experiences, you won't make a good investigator. However, you must also believe paranormal experiences do occur. Today, collecting evidence impartially and then analyzing it to obtain a grounded conclusion is a good approach, rather than starting with a preconceived notion and seeking evidence to support it. Solid evidence that is as clear and as unbiased as possible is crucial to a professional investigation.

97. Evidence Standards: Applying Scientific Methodology

Parapsychologists apply scientific methodology to psychic phenomena. Of course, this approach sometimes annoys not only the skeptics, but also those who are already convinced of the veracity of supernatural phenomena. The skeptics call it pseudoscience, and those already convinced wonder why time is being wasted trying to prove phenomena they have already accepted into their worldview.

Paranormal investigators who follow a scientific methodology seem quite satisfied to keep a foot in both worlds. They feel that in the end, they are doing a real service to believers in the paranormal. They are seeking irrefutable evidence of ghosts, hauntings, and other related events.

Although skeptics loudly proclaim that there is no evidence that any paranormal phenomena is real, plenty of statistically significant evidence has been gathered to support the assertion that remote viewing, precognition, and telepathy all exist.

Be aware that clients may be seeking to debunk you, in their turn. Andrew Laird, founder of The Rhode Island Paranormal Research Group (T.R.I.P.R.G.), was once urgently summoned to a location to do an investigation only to discover that the client had set him up by concealing devices around the premises to simulate a haunting in order to test the group. This has happened to many groups, and most investigators should be aware that it might eventually happen to them, which can impact your credibility if not discovered and exposed. Laird's group discovered the chicanery though the use of listening devices, which detected the sound of the equipment in operation.

Keep high evidence standards in mind when evaluating data.

98. Using the Internet for Research and Promotion

The Internet presents a wonderful smorgasbord of supernatural sites for eager paranormal investigators. There has been an explosion of interest in all things paranormal, the like of which hasn't been seen since the Victorian era. You can often access background and land-data information via the web. Online parapsychology classes are available, and all sorts of free educational resources exist. Many paranormal investigators have created their own websites.

Because there is so much information so freely available, you must proceed with caution, as with any sort of online research.

Some resources you can access are:

+ Ghost-hunting groups
+ Paranormal/supernatural sites
+ Ghost and haunting photo galleries
+ Free educational sites
+ Marketplaces for ghost-hunting technology and supplies
+ Online paranormal investigation classes
+ Online paranormal bookstores

Shadowlands (*www.ghosthunting101.com*) has some great links for finding paranormal investigative groups in your area. It also has a list of recommended groups. This list is made up of paranormal investigators throughout the United States. The Rhode Island Paranormal Research Group site (*www.triprg.com*) also has a great deal of information and hosts an online forum.

If you're running a paranormal investigation team and you don't have a website, chances are the groups in your area who do have one are getting all the attention and referrals. It may not be strictly necessary when you're first starting out, but once you have become established and have been doing active investigations for about a year, it is time to start seriously thinking about your web presence. Every ghost-hunting group should have a website, for these reasons:

+ It attracts new clients.
+ It attracts fellow paranormal enthusiasts who may want to find and join your group.
+ It allows local media to find you if they want to do an interview on the paranormal.
+ It gives members a place to interact and exchange information online.
+ It can serve as an educational tool on paranormal topics for the community.
+ You can offer classes and workshops.
+ It allows clients to contact you via e-mail.

So many groups are now on the web that yours may not be the first group in the area to go online. That's not bad news; there are plenty of ghosts to go around. A check of other groups' websites will help you in several ways. It will show you what they are doing, and you'll also have the opportunity to note what they aren't doing. Grab a pencil and paper and make notes about the websites for any groups in your region. What is likeable about them? What are they lacking?

These sites have links to many ghost-related website directories and are a good way to check out a lot of sites in a short amount of time:

- *www.dmoz.org/society/paranormal/ghosts/personal_pages*
- *www.google.com/alpha/Top/Society/Paranormal/Ghosts/Personal_Pages*

Even the most rudimentary website is better than no website at all. If you cannot afford a web designer, build your own site. Be sure to maintain and update the site frequently. Include your contact information and an assurance of confidentiality, and mention there will be no charge for your services. Testimonials can boost your credibility as well.

While a website may seem like a total extravagance, it's an absolute necessity. If you can't afford an elaborate site, start small and build it up over time. Even if your site only has your contact information and a little bit of text that states your policies, it is better than no web presence at all. If you are a nonprofit organization, the cost of starting and operating the website may be tax deductible.

99. The Importance of Networking

Make no mistake, psychic researchers are not just about gazing into crystal balls or reading the Tarot anymore. They are all about data compilation and employing standardized procedures to gather data. A network of loosely affiliated organizations around the world gathers evidence of an afterlife and correlates the data to identify patterns and quantifiable facts. If in the process they sometimes seem to be discarding evidence that at one time would have been saved and evaluated, it is only in the name of being scrupulous and thorough.

Organizations have the means to communicate quickly over the Internet. Groups can and do share evidence they have gathered during an investigation and receive input on the analysis of it. Digital files stream over servers and vast quantities of data are analyzed by many sets of eyes and ears, virtually simultaneously.

Such collaborations are usually productive, but occasionally friction over analyses or methodology will drive a wedge between groups.

The Atlantic Paranormal Society (TAPS) is a good example of such collaborations. On its website, it lists its affiliates, which are called "TAPS Family Members," in areas all over the United States. The website says the criteria for being a TAPS Family Member are quite stringent. To be a member of the TAPS Family, an affiliation of paranormal researchers worldwide, you must have been in business for at least one year, have a website, have community references, and accept no payment for your services. Also, the group must be in an area where they need coverage.

100. Sharing and Expanding Your Knowledge

With a few years of ghost hunting and paranormal investigating under your belt, you will be a walking encyclopedia of all things supernatural. You may decide that you wish to share that knowledge with the public and offer presentations, lectures, and classes.

You may be invited to speak at events. If your schedule permits, it is a very good way to increase exposure for your organization and talk about the fundamental approaches used by today's ghost hunters. Don't let shyness or reticence cause you to miss the opportunity to do so; it dramatically increases the whole organization's profile. Try the team approach. If you think you will get stage fright, ask two other team members to provide mutual support and backup.

A survey of ghost-hunting organizations shows that most are asked to talk about their most exciting investigation, particularly if it was local. People love to hear about haunted locations right in their own communities.

If your team has had a particularly active case that is not confidential, bring along pictures, EVP, and any other evidence you were able to gather, such as thermal images or video recordings. Put together a PowerPoint presentation so the audience can see what you're talking about. Even if you must keep the client's identity confidential, you can change names and choose evidence that preserves the client's anonymity. People also love to hear about the whole scientific approach to the investigation and the logistics involved in deploying the teams and equipment.

Many organizations defray their operating costs with supplemental events such as speaking engagements and paranormal classes and workshops. Although most investigators have extremely busy schedules, the revenue from these workshops can help buy new equipment and pay for travel expenses.

A good class or workshop should start with the fundamentals, from the first contact with the clients all the way through a step-by-step description of an investigation and the criteria used to gather hard evidence. One or two instructors can teach the sessions, which can range from entry-level to advanced classes. Sometimes, a particularly promising student is asked to join the organization.

A typical advanced class might be about EVP, orbs, or infrared imaging. An advanced EVP class would cover the basic theory, how to apply it in the field, and what to do with the files to clean them up for evidence review. A course in digital photography for ghost hunters might discuss the basics of operating a digital camera, particularly under low-light shooting conditions, as well as using software programs such as Photoshop Elements to clean up the photos. Also vital would be a discussion of the proper resolution, size, and format for the photos and how to archive them safely.

Even if you're currently a paranormal researcher, learning new skills or developing ones you already possess is also important. Many groups have established psychic-development educational programs for their members. Hands-on training is a great way to develop latent psychic abilities and benefit from the tutelage of seasoned investigators. The experienced investigators have made their own mistakes and can help a novice steer clear of them. The neophytes who observe the more experienced psychic's handling of delicate situations can learn what to do and, perhaps more importantly, what not to do.

For those looking to advance their knowledge and expertise, there are many resources available on the Internet, including online classes. Private classes and personal instruction can also be helpful. Most experts agree that you should read a lot and talk to people with some background in the area in order to put a reading list together. After several weeks of research and reading, you should be able to discern your proper course of action. The important thing to remember is that you have to trust your own instincts and approach the topic with a certain healthy skepticism. Getting personal recommendations from friends or reliable sources is usually the best way to proceed. If you seek out personal instruction, check references and pick someone who has a proven track record of reliability.

101. Beyond Seeking Evidence of the Supernatural

Currently, paranormal investigators hold themselves to a rigorous standard. Their aim is to collect not only personal experiences, but also hard, scientific proof of the existence of ghosts.

But should this always be the primary objective of the group? What about the people who need a resolution to the problems haunting them? Aren't they entitled to some closure? The paranormal organization that is using the public merely to prove the existence of ghosts is not serving the community as well as it could be. Gathering evidence should never be done at the expense of people in distress. Sure, it is the way some groups approach the situation, but in the final analysis, the field should always be about finding a compassionate solution to an intolerable situation.

There will be times when a group is called in to do an investigation simply to validate what is occurring. The client may be the proprietor of a commercial establishment that has a long history of paranormal doings; he may even have adopted the ghost as his mascot and feel that its presence gives a certain cachet to the premises. A paranormal team entering the site operates by certain standards, which should be explained to the client at the point of the initial meeting. Even if the client is okay with the ghost being there, does the ghost feel the same? In the case of residual hauntings, there is no actual interaction between the entity and the observers, so there is really no way to establish whether the entity wants to be released from the site.

However, in the case of interactive hauntings, where the investigators have EVPs and there is a possibility of communication, every attempt should be made to do so. This will often mean bringing in sensitives to try to establish contact. If they are successful at doing so and learn that the spirit or spirits want to go into the light, they should feel an obligation to help them do so, whether the proprietor agrees or not.

In the case of truly scary hauntings, the residents of a house are in dire need of help, and the investigators should do everything in their power to bring relief to the victims of malevolent hauntings. These cases aren't too frequent, but when they do occur, they test everything the group has learned. These cases test the team in ways an ordinary ghost hunt never can. The investigation of a poltergeist or malevolent case requires a different skill set from the average haunting. It is both frightening and exhilarating for the team. To the client, however, it may be just plain terrifying.

People who are desperate to rid themselves of entities that are plaguing them are usually the most motivated clients. Keeping that in mind is an important aspect of the case, and helping them find relief should become the team's number one goal.

Appendix A
MOST HAUNTED
SITES IN AMERICA

The Alamo
San Antonio, Texas

Bell Witch Cave
Adams, Tennessee

Belcourt Castle
Newport, Rhode Island

Lincoln Theater
Decatur, Illinois

Waverly Hills Sanatorium
Louisville, Kentucky

Moore Home / Ax Murder House
Villisca, Iowa

Lemp Mansion
St. Louis, Missouri

Bachelor's Grove
Midlothian, Illinois

Gettysburg Battlefield
Southern Pennsylvania

Alcatraz
San Francisco, California

Castle Hill Inn & Resort
Newport, RI

Winchester Mansion
San Jose, California

Myrtles Plantation
St. Francisville, Louisiana

Bobby Mackey's Music World
Wilder, Kentucky

Old Slave House
Junction, Illinois

The White Horse Tavern
Newport, RI

Appendix B
FAMOUS GHOSTS

Jean Harlow – The blonde bombshell actress who died at the age of 26.

Harry Houdini – His ghost is said to haunt the Plaza Hotel in Las Vegas.

Thomas Ince – One of the most respected directors of the silent film era.

Andrew Jackson – The seventh President of the United States.

Jesse James – Outlaw and train robber.

Thomas Jefferson – The third President of the United States.

Robert E. Lee – Confederate General in the Civil War.

John Lennon – Former Beatle.

Liberace – Known for his piano playing skills, charisma, and diamonds.

Abraham Lincoln – The most often seen spirit of an American President.

Marilyn Monroe – Actress who died mysteriously in 1962.

Elvis Presley – Has been seen by stagehands at the Las Vegas Hilton.

George Reeves – The star of the 1950s TV series *Superman*.

Betsy Ross – Credited with sewing the first American flag.

Bugsy Siegel – A colorful Las Vegas underworld figure.

Dylan Thomas – A Welsh poet and writer.

Mark Twain – Popular humorist, novelist, and writer.

Rudolph Valentino – One of the greatest Hollywood romantic idols.

John Wayne – Seen on his old yacht, the *Wild Goose*.

Orson Welles – Considered one of Hollywood's greatest directors.

Appendix C
GLOSSARY

Akashic Records:
The concept of a vast psychic record of all thoughts and emotions, some human, some not, which is sometimes accessible to advanced souls.

Amulet:
A symbolic magical object imbued with energy, meant to protect its wearer from harm—usually a necklace, ring, or pendant.

Angel:
A non-human entity, a winged celestial being, usually benevolent and kind and possessed of powers and knowledge beyond human comprehension.

Anomaly:
An occurrence for which there is seemingly no normal explanation.

Apparition:
The projection or manifestation of a paranormal being.

Astral Plane:
A dimensional plane at a higher vibration than the earthly plane, where entities both good and bad can be encountered during astral travel in the astral body.

Aura:
An energy field that surrounds the physical body and is
a reflection of the astral body, which can be influenced by
thought and emotion.

Banishing:
A ceremonial, magical ritual to cast out negative energy and
influences. It can refer either to a spiritual cleansing of a person or property.

Cleansing:
A ritual in which negative energy and entities are banished
through prayers, which are spoken aloud and may be adapted
to the user's needs.

Clearing:
Synonym for cleansing.

Demonologist:
A person, sometimes clergy, sometimes not, who studies and
banishes demons.

Digital Audio:
Small recorders of good sound quality which can transfer
their files to the computer.

Digital Video:
A video camera whose files can be transferred to a computer.

Dowsing:
A means of locating different substances and energies by the means of two rods, which cross when the energy field that is being searched for is encountered.

Ectoplasm:
An ethereal substance, which supposedly was exuded by the bodies of mediums and could form into objects and entities.

Ectoplasmic Mist:
A substance which forms out of thin air and looks like a thick fog.

Electromagnetic Field (EMF):
Electrical charges, found in varying degrees in anything which uses electricity or generates a magnetic field.

Elemental:
A nature spirit that can be either good or evil.

Entity:
A classification for a disembodied being, which may be a ghost, a spirit, an elemental, or a demon.

EVP:
Electronic Voice Phenomena. An utterance not heard as it is being spoken but is audible later when the recording is played back.

Exorcism:
A ritual performed to drive a devil or demon from the body or the house it is occupying.

Ghost:
A spirit who may or may not have been a living human being or animal, which can sometimes appear to be semi-transparent.

Haunting:
The repeated appearance of ghosts, spirits, or poltergeists.

Hex:
A magical spell, cast to have influence over a person's life, usually used as a curse.

Hypnosis:
A state of altered consciousness, self-induced or through an external agent. Franz Anton Mesmer first popularized this practice which he called Mesmerism.

Instrumental Transcommunication (ITC):
Two-way, real-time communication with spiritual beings. The entities provide advanced technical information through radio, television, VCRs, telephones, and computers.

Intelligent Haunting:
An entity that is aware of the presence of humans and may be interactive.

Levitation:
A rare phenomenon in which objects or persons are lifted or sometimes hurled though the air. Encountered occasionally in cases of poltergeist activity.

K-2 meter:
An EMF meter that measures magnetic and electrical fields and may be recalibrated for paranormal investigative use.

Materialization:
The brief physical appearance of an entity, seen as it is happening.

Matrixing:
Natural tendency for the human mind to try to interpret sensory data into recognizable patterns.

Medium:
A person with the ability to communicate with the dead.

Metaphysics:
The school of philosophical thought which seeks to understand the meaning of existence and the human soul.

MiniDV:
A small version of the camcorder that records and plays MiniDV tapes.

Necromancy:
The art and practice of communicating with the dead to obtain knowledge, either of the future, or other hidden events.

Poltergeist:
The famous "noisy ghost." A rare form of haunting wherein random objects are moved and sounds and speech are produced by unseen entities, which seem to crave attention and recognition. Frequently a child or adolescent is at the center of the phenomena.

Psychokinesis:
A paranormal phenomenon in which objects are moved, solely by the powers of the psychic's mind. See Telekinesis.

Reincarnation:
The belief that a soul will move on to another body after death to work out its karmic debt.

Residual Haunting:
A psychic recording of an event that is traumatic or violent. It is repeated over and over, and the entity involved does not interact with onlookers.

Saging:
See Smudge Sticks.

Séance:
The attempt by a group to contact the spirit world. A medium is usually the channel through which the energies manifest.

Sigil:
A magical charm that forms an energy barrier and protective shield. It can be visualized or drawn.

Smudge Sticks:
A Native American tool made of sage used for purification, healing, and cleansing ceremonies. The smoke is thought to clear negative energies.

Spirit:
A ghost. An entity which once existed on the earthly plane but has passed on.

Synchronicity:
Uncanny coincidences that seem too convenient to be truly coincidental.

Telekinesis:
The psychic phenomenon where objects are moved solely by the mind.

Vortex:

A rip in the fabric of space-time that opens into the spirit world and lets entities from the other side in.

Ward:

A magical construct that guards a person or a place.

Wraith:

The semi-transparent image of a person that appears shortly before or after their death, also sometimes used when talking about a ghost.

Appendix D
BIBLIOGRAPHY

Auerbach, Loyd. *ESP, Hauntings and Poltergeists*. Berkeley, CA: Ronin Publishing, 2004.

Blum, Deborah. *Ghost Hunters: The Victorians and the Hunt for Proof of Life after Death*. City of Westminster, London: Penguin Group, 2006.

Hawes, Jason & Grant Wilson with Michael Jan Friedman. *Ghost Hunting: True Stories of Unexplained Phenomena from The Atlantic Paranormal Society*. New York, NY: Gallery, 2007.

Heinemann, Dr. Klaus and Miceal Ledwith. *The Orb Project*. New York, NY: Atria Books/Beyond Words, 2007.

Jones, Marie D. *PSIence: How New Discoveries in Quantum Physics and New Science May Explain the Existence of Paranormal Phenomena*. Franklin Lakes, NJ: New Page Books, 2006.

Lethbridge, Thomas Charles. *Ghost and Ghoul*. New York, NY: Doubleday, 1962.

Martin, Dr. Malachi. *Hostage to the Devil, The Possession and Exorcism of Five Contemporary Americans*. New York, NY: HarperOne, 1992.

Post, Lauren Van Der. *The Lost World of the Kalahari*. San Diego, CA: Harvest Books, 1977.

Rogo, D. Scott. *The Haunted House Handbook*. New York, NY: Berkeley Publishing Group, 1981.

____ *The Welcoming Silence: A Study of Psychical Phenomena and Survival of Death*. University Books, 1973.

Willin, Dr. Melvyn. *Ghosts Caught on Film: Photographs of the Paranormal*. Newton Abbot, UK: David & Charles, 2007.

Wilson, Colin. *Mysteries: An Investigation into the Occult, the Paranormal & the Supernatural*. New York, NY: Putnam, 1978.

____ *The Occult*. London: Watkins, 2006.

____ *Poltergeist*. Woodbury, MN: Llewellyn Publications, 1995.

Young, Gloria. *Faces of a Ghost Hunter*. Raleigh, NC: Lulu, 2004.

INDEX

Air ion counters, 168
Amazon.com, 9
Amityville Horror, 96, 192
Amulets, 95, 106, 117
Ancestry.com, 45
Animals and pets
    ghosts of, 39
    reactions to hauntings, 124, 128
Apparitions, 26–27, 71
Arrests, avoiding, 132, 139, 142
Astral plane, 88
The Atlantic Paranormal Society
    (TAPS), 10, 73, 75, 105, 108, 206
Attacks. See Physical attacks; Psychic
    attacks
Audacity (program), 77, 159
Audio recorders/recordings, 4, 68, 70,
    154, 157–60, 171
    analog, 172
    cleaning up material, 174
    digital, 172, 174, 175
    preservation and preparation of,
        76, 77
    types of, 159–60
Auerbach, Loyd, 9, 69
Auras, 85
Automatic writing, 88

Barnes, Jeff, 45
Baseline readings, 43, 48
Bathing, ritual, 118
Batteries, 4, 5, 42, 108, 109, 155, 166,
    192
Belcourt Castle, 107–8
Bell family, 29
Benedict XVI, Pope, 113
Biddle, Kenneth, 157
Binding, 30
Black, Kym, 42, 74, 96–97, 104, 107
Black light/UV light, 170

Boleyn, Anne, 36
The Book of the Dead/The Book of Going
    Forth by Day, 25
Broome, Fiona, 11
Buddy system, 6, 17

Cambridge University Museum, 131
Cameras, 5, 42. See also Photographs;
    Thermal imagers/images
    capturing elusive images, 176–77
    digital, 10, 154, 156–57, 191, 208
    infrared, 161–62
    malfunctions in, 109
    raw format files, 157
Candles and matches, 5, 42, 108
Carpenter, William, 89
Case files, 57
Case managers, 43, 124, 126, 182–83
Case numbers, 77
Catholicism, 96, 112–14
CDs, 76, 77–79
Cell phones, 4–5, 42, 130, 142
Cemeteries, 34, 59, 132, 134, 141
Charms, 116–17
Children
    ensuring security of, 124
    frightening, avoiding, 136
    interviewing, 127
    poltergeists and, 15, 28
City (reverse) directories, 143
Clairaudience, 85
Claircognizance, 84–85
Clairsentience, 84
Clairvoyance, 85
Classes, workshops, and seminars,
    10–12, 198, 207–9
Cleansing, 55, 68, 117–21, 198
    house, 119–21
    personal, 118
Clergy, 112–14

Client questionnaires, 138
Clients
 confidentiality and privacy (*see*
  Confidentiality; Privacy, client)
 educating and comforting, 54–56
 integrity and accountability to,
  57–59
 interviewing (*see* Interviews)
 problematic, 107–8
 responsibility of, 63–64
 showing data to, 59–60
 walk-through and site check with,
  43–46
Client summary reports, 138
Closed-circuit TV, 169
Clothing
 ghost-hunting, 170–71
 for meeting potential clients, 141
Coincidence, 6, 82–83
Cold spots, 32–33, 35, 38, 124, 128, 154,
 160. *See also* Temperature anomalies
Collective unconscious, 87
Compasses, 167
Computers, laptop, 155
Confidentiality, 51–54, 136, 181, 207
 in practical terms, 51
 release from, 53–54, 140
Confidentiality agreements, 52–53, 57,
 137, 138, 144
 sample, 53
Congregation for the Doctrine of the
 Faith, 113
Courthouses and city halls, 143–44
Crystal balls, 87
Cyndislist.com, 45

Dean, James (cursed Porsche of),
 110–11
 Debunking, 17, 70, 71–72, 129, 198,
  201, 202

Demonologists, 192–93
Demons, 30, 62–63, 192–93. *See also*
 Exorcisms
 characteristics and behavior of,
  27–28
 protection against, 96, 106
Devil's Den, 37
Digital media. *See also* Audio recorders/
 recordings, digital; Cameras, digital;
 Thermometers, digital
 controversy over, 156–57
 storage of, 77–79
 types of, 154
Digital video recorders/recordings
 (DVRs), 7, 33, 42, 154
Digital voice recorders (DVRs), 159
Disclose.tv, 32
Divination, 87, 99
Dmoz.org, 205
Dowsing, 89–92, 99
Dowsing rods, 5, 34
Dreams, frightening, 101, 128
Drug and alcohol use, avoiding, 58
Dust masks, 155
DVDs, 76, 77–79
DVRs. *See* Digital video recorders/
 recordings; Digital voice recorders

Ectoplasm, 31–32
Edison, Thomas, 172
Education
 client, 54–56
 self-, 8–11, 207–9
Electromagnetic field (EMF), 4, 31, 33,
 109, 129, 167
Electromagnetic frequency (EMF)
 meters, 4, 5, 10, 154, 162–66
 site conditions influencing, 44, 45,
  46, 130
 types of, 163–65

Electromagnetic smog signature, 164
Electronic voice phenomena (EVP),
    6, 9, 10, 35, 54, 59, 74, 157–60,
    171–74, 208
    characteristics of, 158
    discovery of, 171–72
    steps to record, 173
Elementals, 29–30, 106
ELF meters. See Extremely low
    frequency meters
EMF. See Electromagnetic field
EMF/gauss meters, 165
EMF meters. See Electromagnetic
    frequency meters
Eno, Paul F., 31
Environmental worksheets, 45
Epinephrine, stocking, 148
Equipment, 153–77. See also specific
    types
    checking and deploying, 46–47
    double checking, 42
    essential list, 3–5
    failure, common causes of, 155
    failure, guarding against, 108–9
    general advice on, 154–56
    insuring, 150–51
    low-tech, 166–67
    miscellaneous, 167–70
    site conditions influencing, 129–30
Equipment managers, 46, 183–84
ESP. See Extrasensory perception
ESP, Hauntings and Poltergeists
    (Auerbach), 9
The Everything Psychic Book
    (Hathaway), 81
Evidence, 67–79. See also Scientific
    method
    analyzing, 70–71
    beyond seeking of, 209–11
    evaluating, 68–69

hard vs. personal experiences,
    69–70
    preservation and preparation of,
    76–77
    what to look for, 71–72
Evidence release or no release forms,
    138
Evidence review findings, 139
EVP. See Electronic voice phenomena
Exorcisms, 55–56, 103, 105, 112–14
The Exorcist (film), 111, 113
Extra-high frequency (EHF) sounds,
    169
Extrasensory perception (ESP), 24,
    83, 196
Extremely low frequency (ELF) meters,
    162, 165, 169
Eyewitness accounts, collecting, 48–50

Facial-composite software, 155
Fairy rings, 110
Familysearch.org, 45
Feralia, 26
Financial matters
    cost of entering field, 197
    defraying operating costs, 208
    free services, 64, 206
    income from ghost hunting, 195,
    196–98
First-aid kits, 4, 42, 147–48, 187
Flamel College, 11
Flashlights, 4, 42, 166
Florio, Maggie, 74, 174, 190
Follow-up, 43, 61
Follow-up questionnaires, 138
Forms, 137–39. See also Confidentiality
    agreements; Permission to
    investigate, forms; Release forms
Fortune, Dion, 34
Fu Ji, 88

Garuda Purana, 25
Gauss, Karl Friedrich, 164
Gauss meters, 164, 165
Gauss multi-detectors, 164
Geiger counters, 169
Geller, Uri, 90
Genealogy research, 44–45
Geocoder.us, 70
Gettysburg battlefield, 32, 37
Ghost and Ghoul (Lethbridge), 35
Ghost boxes, 175–76
Ghost hunters, 195–211
    financial matters (*see* Financial
        matters)
    methodology and, 200–201 (*see also*
        Scientific method)
    networking and, 205–6
    objectivity and, 3, 57, 64–65
    primary objectives of, 209–11
    professionalism and, 57, 64–65
    qualities exemplified by, 2–3
    reputation, maintaining,
        199–200
    sharing and expanding knowledge,
        207–9
    tips for, 1–2
Ghost Hunters (television program), 10,
    30, 54, 75, 108–9, 201
Theghosthunterstore.net, 156
Ghost-hunting equipment. *See*
    Equipment
Ghosthunting101.com, 203
Ghost Research Society, 88
Ghosts
    in ancient cultures, 23, 24–26
    appearance and characteristics of,
        26–27
    common manifestation sites, 34
    communication by, 34–35
    famous, 217–19

percentage of Americans believing
    in, 23–24
poltergeists compared with, 28
substance of, 31–32
Ghoststudy.com, 192
Ghostvillage.com, 156
Ghouls, 103
Groupthink, 83–84

Hair, tying back, 42, 58
Hardwire thermometers, 160–61
Hathaway, Michael R., 81
Haunted House Handbook (Rogo), 9
Haunted sites. *See* Sites
Hawes, Jason, 105, 162
Hexes, 109–11
Historians, local, 135
Historical societies, 133
Hoaxes, 49, 86, 170, 182. *See also*
    Debunking; Scams
Hobby, ghost hunting as, 155, 195–211.
    See also Ghost hunters
Hollow Hill, 11
Holy water, 96
Homeowners' associations, obtaining
    information from, 143
Human hauntings, intelligent, 30,
    38–39

Ideomotor action, 89
Infrared cameras, 161–62
Infrared thermometers, 160
Infrasonic sound, 67–68
Inhuman hauntings, 30, 39, 193
Instinct *vs.* intellect, 19–21
Insurance, 150–51
Intelligent hauntings, 30, 38–39
Internet
    classes on, 10–11, 203
    ghost-hunting products on, 175

Internet—*continued*
  members-only websites, 198
  paranormal research groups on, 13
  promotion via, 203–5
  research on, 10, 134, 135, 144, 196,
    203–5
Interviews, 48–50
  forms for, 138
  on-site, 126–29
Intuition, 82–83
Investigation reports, 139, 184–85
Investigations, 123–51. *See also* Clients;
  Legalities; Research; Sites
  assessing need for, 56
  assessing threat level, 125–26
  common-sense checklist, 42
  dos and don'ts, 58–59
  extended and repeat, 62–63
  follow-up to, 43, 61
  handling requests, 124–25
  percentage with paranormal activity,
    64
  rules of conduct, 58
Investigators private report, 139

Jackson, Andrew, 29
Jinxes, 109–11
John XXIII, Pope, 97
Journeys Out of the Body (Monroe), 98
Jürgenson, Friedrich, 171–72

Kaczmarek, Dale, 88
Keyport Paranormal, 176
Kinesthesia, 188
K2 EMF meters, 163

Laird, Andrew, 104, 112–13, 202
Lanterns, kerosene, 5, 42, 166
Legalities, 132–33, 137, 139, 141, 142
Lemuria, 25–26

Leo XIII, Pope, 97
Lethbridge, Thomas Charles, 35–36, 131
Ley lines, 34, 131
Liability, 52, 137, 139, 145
  release from, 140
Library research, 133–34, 135
Light, crossing into, 56, 210
Lightning, effects of, 165
Lizzie Borden Bed and Breakfast, 54
Location history forms, 139
Logs, 47, 68, 70, 139
  steps for keeping, 8
  teamwork in, 184–86
The Lost World of the Kalahari (van der
  Post), 109–10

Magnetic anomaly detectors, 5
Magnetic field sensors, 167–68
Malevolent entities, 95, 98–99,
  103, 210–11. *See also* Demons;
  Elementals
Map dowsing. *See* Dowsing
Maps, 5
Marconi, Guglielmo, 158
Martin, Malachi, 113–14
Matrixing anomalies, 72–74
Media consultants, 198
Medical information and preparedness,
  146–50
Meditation, 2, 87, 96–97
Mediums, 31
Mental health practitioners, 55,
  63
Mental stability, 14–15, 49, 112
Michael, St. (invoking), 97–98
Microcassettes, 159
Mists and fogs, 32–34, 71, 74
Mobile weather stations, 63
Money. *See* Financial matters
Monroe, Robert, 98

Murder (on site), 133, 162
Mysteries (Wilson), 8

National Register of Historical Places, 144
Necromancy, 87–89
Neighbors, obtaining information from, 136, 142–43
Networking, 205–6
Night-vision devices, 161, 169
Nostradamus, 92
Notebooks, 4
Notes, 6–7, 68

Observer effect, 65
The Occult (Wilson), 9
Om imprint, 24–25
Orbs, 33, 71, 74, 108, 156, 168, 176–77
Ouija boards, 88, 99, 127, 128, 172

Paine House, 104
Paranormal investigators. *See* Ghost hunters
Parapsychological Association, 193
Parapsychologists, 192–93
Parentalia, 26
Pendulums, 2, 5, 87, 90–91
Permission-free sites, 146
Permission to investigate forms, 58, 138, 139–41, 142, 145
obtaining, 132–33, 141–45, 186
Petit, Nelia, 96, 100, 104
Phone calls from the dead (PCFTD), 158–59
Photographs, 68, 70, 71. *See also* Cameras
authentication of, 156–57
preservation and preparation of, 76
reviewing and evaluating, 32–34, 74–75

tips for photographers, 191–92
Photoshop Elements (program), 76, 208
Physical attacks, 104–7, 187
Plants, negative energy absorbed by, 117
Police, communicating with, 143, 146
Poltergeist (Wilson), 8
Poltergeists, 16, 17, 26, 39, 88, 95, 108, 131, 154–55, 169, 211
characteristics and behavior of, 28–29
physical attacks by, 105
Pontefract Poltergeist, 131
Poseyghosts.wordpress.com, 45
Possession, 103, 105, 111–12. *See also* Exorcisms
Prairieghosts.com, 9
Prayer, 96, 98, 106, 118
Precognition, 196
Priests, 112–14
Privacy, client, 50, 51–52
Professional ghost hunters. *See* Ghost hunters
Property damage, 132, 137, 139–40, 145
Protection and self-defense, 30–31, 95–121. *See also* Cleansing; Safety; Visualization
from attacks and oppression, 99–107
basics of, 96–97
invoking St. Michael, 97–98
from jinxes and hexes, 109–11
priests and clergy in, 112–14
sigils and charms in, 116–18
wards and shields in, 114–16
Psychic attacks, 99–102, 187
Psychic oppression, 102–3
Psychics, 85–87, 18⁻

Psychic skills, 81–93. *See also* specific skills
  developing, 82–83
Psychic skills—*continued*
  theories on source of, 83–84
  types of, 84–85
Psychokinesis (PK), 28, 65, 196
Psychometry, 196

Quantum matter, 30–31

Raths, 110
Record keeping
  correct methodology, 48
  importance of accuracy, 6–9
  manual, 47–48
  the scientific method and, 17
  teamwork in, 184–86
Reincarnation, 24–25
Release forms, 139–41, 145
  sample, 149–50
  types of, 140
Religious opinions, avoiding expression of, 14
Remote sensor wireless thermometers, 160
Remus, 26
Reports, 184–86
Research
  Internet, 10, 134, 135, 144, 196, 203–5
  resources and tips, 131–37, 142–44
  ~rch groups, paranormal, 13–15
      ~ntings, 27, 30, 35–37, 95,

            ~al Research
              ~ 96,

       ~6~

Richet, Charles, 31
Rogo, D. Scott, 9
Rosaries, 96
Rubber cement, 5
Ruff Stone Tavern, 75

Safety, 186–87. *See also* Medical information and preparedness; Protection and self-defense
Saging, 106, 118
Satanism, 113
Scams, 16. *See also* Hoaxes
Scapulars, 96
Schoonover, Nathan, 55
Scientific method, 16–19, 48, 201–2
Scrying, 2, 92–93
Séances, 2, 32, 88, 107–8, 127, 128
Seers, 85–87
Sensitives, 187, 188–91, 210
Shadowlands, 203
Shadow people, 26
Sheldrake, Rupert, 3
Shields, 114–16
Sidereal time, 69–70
Sigils, 116–17
Site-assessment reports, 184–85
Sites
  age of, 44, 124
  gathering information on, 131–33
  hazards in, 43–44
  history of, 44–45, 135–37
  interviews at, 126–29
  layout and location of, 129–31
  most haunted in U.S., 213–15
  permission requirements (*see* Permission entries)
  sources of information on, 133–37
  vacant, 142–44
  walk-through and check, 43–46
Skepticism, 1, 3, 4, 22, 201, 202

Smells associated with hauntings, 35, 75, 124

Smoking, avoiding, 15, 32, 42, 58, 192

Society for Psychical Research (SPR), 20

Sound-level meters, 169–70

Spells, 118

Spiritualist movement, 88

Static electricity, 109

String, black, 5

Strobe lights, mini, 155

Suicidal thoughts, 102, 103

Suicide (on site), 133, 162

Sumption, Frank, 176

Superconscious, 84, 87

Tape measures and yardsticks, 5

Tape recorders. See Audio recorders/recordings

TAPS. See The Atlantic Paranormal Society

Tarot cards, 99

Tassili Najjer, 89

Taylor, Troy, 10, 156

Teams, 179–93

   awareness, responsibility, and safety, 186–87

   building and organizing, 11–13

   leader's accountability to members, 180–82

   reports and, 184–86

Telepathy, 83

Temperature anomalies, 7, 33, 35, 71, 109, 128, 154. See also Cold spots; Thermometers, digital

Tesla, Nikola, 158

Thermal hygrometers, digital, 168

Thermal imagers/images, 34, 70, 71, 76, 77, 162, 167

Thermometers, digital, 7, 11, 35, 70, 154

types of, 160–61

Third eye, 85

TIFFs, 76

Title searches, 144

Tower of London, 37

Trespassing, 132, 139, 142

TriField Natural EM meters, 165

T.R.I.P.R.G. See The Rhode Island Paranormal Research Group

Two-way radios, 168

Tycho.usno.navy.mil, 70

Universal Class, 10–11

Vacant properties, 142–44

Van der Post, Lauren, 109–10

Video recordings, 70, 71, 155, 156–57

   preservation and preparation of, 76–77

   reviewing and evaluating, 74–75

   tips for videographers, 191–92

Visualization, 87, 96, 114–16

Voices From the Universe (Jürgenson), 172

Walkie-talkies, 42, 108, 187

Wards, 114–16

Warren, Ed and Lorraine, 96, 192–93

Watches, 4, 167

Water, effects of, 34, 131

WavePad (program), 77, 174

Weather, effects of, 6, 7, 37, 48, 63, 103, 165, 168

The Welcoming Silence (Rogo), 9

White light, invoking, 96

White noise, 174–76

Wilson, Colin, 8

Wilson, Grant, 73, 108–9, 162

Wireless microphones, 159–60

Writing about the paranormal, 198

BEYOND HERE

Sure, this world is fascinating, but
what's beyond is even more intriguing...

Want a place to share stories and experiences
about all things strange and unusual? From
UFOs and apparitions to dream interpre-
tation, the Tarot, astrology, and more, the
BEYOND HERE blog is the newest hot spot for
paranormal activity!

Sign up for our newsletter at
www.adamsmedia.com/blog/paranormal
and download our free Haunted U.S. Hot Spots Map!